Jan 2018

To Nanette
with many
and appreciation
for your wonderful
work —
Always,
Leora
Evans

THE EVOLVING

Peacemaker

A COMMITMENT TO NONVIOLENCE

BY
LEONA EVANS

WITH
MATTHEW J. EVANS

FOREWORD BY ARUN GANDHI

BALBOA.
PRESS

A DIVISION OF HAY HOUSE

Balboa Press books may be ordered through booksellers or by contacting:

Balboa Press
A Division of Hay House
1663 Liberty Drive
Bloomington, IN 47403
www.balboapress.com
1 (877) 407-4847

Cover Art: Linda Mercer

Print information available on the last page.

ISBN: 978-1-5043-7079-0 (sc)
ISBN: 978-1-5043-7080-6 (hc)
ISBN: 978-1-5043-7104-9 (e)

Library of Congress Control Number: 2016920052

Balboa Press rev. date: 07/26/2017

*For Carol Keefer (1939–2004), whose unconditional
love has made an indelible impact on our lives.*

Contents

Foreword

Arun Gandhi

O n a flight to Europe for a conference on nonviolence, I found myself seated next to a self-styled guru of nonviolent political action. I prefer to shroud him in anonymity, to save both of us embarrassment. Suffice it to say that he is a graduate of Harvard University, who did a doctoral thesis on nonviolence.

I think he was intimidated by my presence; he became aggressive from the start. When I told him I would like to talk about nonviolence, he retorted: "Nonviolence is nothing but a strategy of convenience. Don't try to bring in any spiritual hocus-pocus."

Spiritual hocus-pocus is, of course, a debatable point. Spirituality to him obviously meant religious connection, whereas spirituality to me means having faith in your belief and, especially, in the pursuit of truth. It is difficult to believe in and practice a philosophy if you have no faith in it. I agree that nonviolence is not exclusive to any one religion, nor does it require the infusion of any religious rituals. It belongs to every religion, and people from every religion have practiced nonviolence for centuries.

Gandhi admitted that nonviolence is "as old as the hills" and that he applied it in the political context because it was the most civilized and sensible thing to do. But he also said that the more he thought about it and the more he applied it, the more profound it became. The philosophy of nonviolence is like the proverbial iceberg. What is still hidden from our knowledge is tens of times more than what we know.

It was this revelation that made Gandhi believe that nonviolence is more than just a strategy—it has to be a way of life. Not only is it impractical to be nonviolent one moment and violent the next or to practice both violence and nonviolence simultaneously, but this way of thinking ignores the fact that we humans practice violence in many more ways than just wars and street fighting but in ways that often we don't even think of as being violent. Who would have thought, for instance, that wasting food or tolerating poverty are the worst forms of violence? But they are.

If our words or behavior hurts someone, then that is violence. It could be direct or indirect violence. If our lavish lifestyle can only be sustained by exploiting people or resources of the world, then that is exploitation and, therefore, violence. In short, to maintain a materialistic economy, we have created an oppressive *culture of violence* that dominates and controls every aspect of our lives. Our language, sports, entertainment, music, relationships—in fact, everything about us—is violent, because everything is nurtured by selfishness and greed.

In this milieu of violence, working to end wars or fighting in city streets is like attempting to douse a fire with water while feeding it with oil at the same time. The fire flares or abates depending on which pump works the hardest. We are not aware that this dance of violence is like cancer that is slowly and imperceptibly destroying our humanity. When that happens, there is very little hope for civilization to survive. History is replete with stories of ancient civilizations that perished because of arrogance.

When fifteen-year-old Matthew J. Evans approached me for an interview for a film, my first reaction was based in arrogance. What would a fifteen-year-old understand about nonviolence? Then I remembered my grandfather's prophetic words: "If we are going to create peace in the world, we will have to begin with educating children." Indeed, only they can become the change we wish to see in this world. So I grabbed the opportunity to speak to him on video. Matthew is not only sensitive but wise beyond his years. He understood the essence of what I was saying and projected it so effectively in his film that he has won awards and, hopefully, changed lives. He has the distinction of changing the life of his mother, Rev. Leona Evans. Both the son and the mother have become champions of nonviolence. Rev. Leona has put into this book everything that Matthew put into his film—and more. This book will take humanity another step closer to peace and harmony in our world.

As an evolving peacemaker,

I reach out to embrace all life,

with hope for the future

and an ongoing commitment

to help establish

a culture of peace in our world

one person at a time ...

beginning with me.

Introduction

Creating a Culture of Peace

The Evolving Peacemaker, based on the Gandhi philosophy of nonviolence, contains a set of principles and practices designed to guide us on a powerful journey of self-discovery and enlightenment. It opens with the premise that peace is not a one-time achievement but a lifelong practice that starts with our willingness to "be the change we wish to see in our world," one thought and one action at a time.

Mohandas (Mahatma) Gandhi's own life and his visions for a culture of peace are legendary. His courage and perseverance in the face of adversity have inspired people from all walks of life. Although he had many reasons to feel discouraged, Gandhi never lost his faith in the goodness and resilience of the human spirit to find a path to higher ground.

In these troubled times we also have reasons to feel discouraged and disheartened. However, for the sake of our children and the future of our planet, we cannot afford to give up or cave in. It is time for nonviolence to prevail and for you and I to prepare ourselves to lead the way.

In the following chapters we will become familiar with the Gandhi teachings and work with effective methods designed to awaken us to the possibilities of embracing a culture of peace. We will learn to enhance the quality of our relationships by working with Gandhi's four concepts of respect, understanding, acceptance, and appreciation. We will shed light on the nature of anger, work to recognize and heal passive violence within ourselves, explore the power of forgiveness, and come to understand that Gandhi's vision of nonviolence involves much more than nonaction.

A Personal Quest for Peace

I have also included aspects of my own commitment to nonviolence, which began one day when I was eleven years old. It marked the first of many occasions when I was attacked and bullied because of my religious beliefs. Those early struggles motivated me to study the history of world religions in an effort to understand why so many acts of violence have been committed in the name of God. Eventually I chose the ministry as a way of helping people see that nonviolence among religions begins with the realization that the same God of love indwells all people. It was during this time that I first read Gandhi's book *The Way to God* and was deeply impressed with his inclusive and benevolent approach to spirituality.

The Evolving Peacemaker also contains stories of my meetings with Arun Gandhi and his gracious participation in a touching documentary short film that my son, Matthew J. Evans, produced when he was sixteen years old. The film was my inspiration for writing this book, and Arun's valuable contributions throughout this volume have helped bring the Gandhi philosophy to life in loving and insightful ways.

In addition, you will find a chapter authored by Matthew in which he describes his experience at the United Nations, where he received an important award for his film. In subsequent chapters, he shares significant shifts in his own consciousness as part of his personal quest for peace and contributes fascinating scientific data on the interrelatedness of all life.

Matthew is a most loving presence in my life and I see in him a highly gifted and powerful soul who inspires me and everyone who knows him with a vision of hope for our future.

Focusing on the Journey

Our mission as evolving peacemakers is to do all we can to help shift the consciousness of our planet from a culture of violence to a culture of peace. It is a process that requires patience, persistence, and the willingness to see ourselves and all of humanity as a sacred work in progress. This involves learning to focus our energies on the journey rather than the destination.

We live in a world of beginnings and endings. When one project is finished, we move on to another. We are constantly encouraged to be goal oriented and to finish our tasks in a punctual manner. We are accustomed to feeling a sense of satisfaction when we contribute our time and energy to a project that comes to fruition.

On the other hand, when things seem to be taking too long, we can find ourselves becoming anxious and frustrated because we want to see the finished product. We turn to those around us and ask, "Who is responsible for getting this done?" or "Why isn't this happening faster?"

These are appropriate questions to ask when we know what the finished product is supposed to look like. Our quest for peace, however, is much more than a task with a beginning and an end. It is an abstract, spiritual process of discovering who we are, why we are here, and how we can honor our relationship with all creation. It involves an ongoing series of trials and errors, growth and overcoming, and awakening to new insights only to forget them until we learn again and again. It is figuring out how to use words instead of weapons, developing an intimate relationship with our spiritual powers, and finding ways to use them wisely.

Peace in our world involves learning to have respectful and ethical relations with those of other countries, interacting wisely with one another in business, respecting each other's cultures and unique ways of living, and realizing that in a win-lose system *everyone* loses. It is learning to make wise choices and coming to see that just because we are able to do something doesn't necessarily mean we should.

Peace is a process of learning to reach out to all people as equals, emphasizing our commonalities and honoring our differences, developing the ability to agree to disagree, finding ways to forgive, and helping to alleviate suffering. It is looking for new ways to feed the hungry and working diligently to replenish our natural resources.

We ask, "Who is responsible for getting this done?" The answer is inescapable: "It begins with me."

"Why isn't this happening faster?"

Creating a culture of peace is an enormous undertaking, which involves doing everything we can to remember our purpose and stay centered on our goals. Spending too much time and energy finding fault with others for not making it happen faster only creates more chaos in our environment and takes us further away from the peace we are seeking.

Our real works lies in shifting our attention from fear and frustration to finding practical solutions to our problems and respecting the process itself. This is how we can nurture and support the sacred ideal of peace. By embracing these values and incorporating them into our daily lives, we become *evolving peacemakers.*

Defining a Culture of Peace

A culture of peace is more than the absence of conflict; it is a way of life that includes multiple levels of participation. According to the *United Nations Declaration on a Culture of Peace* adopted by the General Assembly in September of 1999, this includes respect for all life, an end to discrimination, promotion of equal rights, meeting developmental and environmental needs for present and future generations, eliminating all forms of discrimination, ensuring protection for the rights of children, eradicating poverty and illiteracy, and reducing inequalities among nations. A culture of peace involves educational reform and adherence to the principles of freedom, justice, democracy, acceptance, cultural diversity, and understanding at all levels.

Who can participate in a culture of peace? Parents; teachers; corporations; politicians; small businesses; journalists and other media; religious organizations; those engaged in scientific, philosophical, creative, and artistic activities; health and humanitarian workers; social workers; retired people; and nongovernmental organizations. In other words, all of us.

I encourage you to become familiar with the many and varied organizations and movements aimed at developing a culture of peace. Increasing numbers of individuals are making conscious choices to bring deeper levels of compassion and understanding to a world badly in need of healing. There are literally hundreds of groups around the world dedicated to advancing the cause of peace. Rather than listing them here or recommending specific groups, I suggest you seek them out via word of mouth or the Internet. As you search the web, you will find spiritual and educational communities that are inclusive in nature and emphasize nonviolent social action. I highly recommend that you become an active part of the communities that are most meaningful to you.

To all of you who are active in the various peace movements around the globe, I extend my heartfelt thanks for your passion and dedication to this work. Please remember that you are not alone. You are making a tremendous difference toward building a more loving consciousness on this planet, and your work matters. I pray that in this volume you will find meaningful insights and the encouragement to continue blessing others with your important contributions toward a world of peace.

To those of you who desire a better future but are not certain how to begin moving in a positive direction, I trust that the ideas presented in the following pages will inspire you to become an evolving peacemaker.

May we each feel inspired by the unconditional love of Spirit that dwells in us all as we embark upon the journey of a lifetime, doing our part to lift the consciousness of our planet from a culture of violence to a culture of peace.

As an evolving peacemaker,

I walk the path of

new beginnings.

Chapter 1

My First Encounter with Violence

When I was in the sixth grade, I was attacked by a neighborhood teenager, an incident that made an unforgettable impact on my life.

It was a mild, sunny day in my hometown of Chicago, and I was walking home from school thinking about having a snack and hanging out with my friends. I stopped at a street corner and waited for the traffic light to turn green. All of a sudden I heard a loud voice behind me, yelling, "Hey!" I turned my head just as a hard object smashed into my right eye. The impact was so strong it almost knocked me over.

The lens of my thick glasses shattered, and I cried out in pain as the pointed shards of glass lacerated my eyelid and dug into my face. *A rock! Who threw a rock?* Once again the same voice yelled loudly from down the street, and I remembered the big kid from another school who had once shouted insults about my religion. Now here he was again, spewing more religious slurs at me. He shouted, "You have no right to breathe the same air as I do. Your kind would be better off dead!" He threw another rock, and I turned away quickly as it grazed my shoulder. Just then another boy called out to him, and he hopped on his bike and rode away.

For a while I stood very still, and everything became very quiet around me. A couple of people walked by, but they did not look at me or appear to have witnessed what had just happened. For the

1

first time in my life I felt completely alone and very, very ashamed. I thought, *What terrible thing have I done for someone to treat me this way?*

Blood trickled down my cheek, and I reached for the handkerchief in my pocket. Carefully I removed what was left of my glasses and gently held the folded cotton cloth to my face while I walked the rest of the way home. When I entered the house and my mother saw me holding a blood-soaked handkerchief over my eye she held back a scream, grabbed her purse, and took me to the nearest hospital.

Shortly after we arrived at the emergency room, a doctor injected me with an anesthetic for the pain and with a tiny instrument deftly extracted bits of glass from around my eye and cheek. After a thorough examination, he told us that I would suffer no permanent damage, and he prescribed antibiotics, topical medication, and two weeks of bed rest.

That evening my parents and grandparents engaged in a long and heated discussion. Of course they were deeply distressed that I had been bullied and assaulted, but mostly they were terrified of responding in a way that would inadvertently cause more harm. This was not their first encounter with religious discrimination, and they knew how quickly these situations could get out of hand. They feared that if they tried to confront the boy's family or chose to involve the police, something even worse might happen to me. The discussion wore on for several hours, until my parents and grandparents finally shook their heads and sadly concluded, "There's nothing we can do. We don't want to make more trouble."

My grandparents held me close and made me promise to always walk to and from school with a group of friends, never by myself. Then they sat with me for a long time without speaking. I could sense their profound disappointment and regret as they accepted the harsh reality that bigotry and intolerance would be a part of my life, just as it had been for them and those who went before them. Finally, they hugged me again, and with tears in their eyes told me how much they loved me and that none of this was my fault.

As I got ready for bed that evening, a deeply disturbing feeling came over me. My world was no longer safe, and I knew for certain that although this was my first real experience with bullying and violence it would not be my last.

Process and Discovery

For the next two weeks, as I lay recuperating on our living-room sofa, my mind was full of questions. I thought, *That kid doesn't even know me—what's his problem with my religion? What's so wrong with people worshipping in different ways?*

Certainly I was aware of the dangers of religious persecution. I had read history books that told of horrible abuses inflicted upon various segments of humanity in the name of God. I suppose I just assumed that many of those issues no longer existed. I thought that people were learning to accept one another in spite of their religious differences, just as we were taught to do in school. I was shocked that this kind of prejudice was still going on, especially among children.

My mind continued to question: *What is God? Where is God? Why are there different religions in the world? Which religion is the right one? Is there a way to find out what God really wants from us?*

At one point I imagined the most unusual scenario of all: *Is it possible that God is playing a game with us, and everyone who goes to the wrong church will be punished for all eternity?*

Although the idea of a vindictive God was frightening at first, I soon began to see the humor in it. I started smiling and then began laughing so hard that my eye started throbbing and I had to settle down. The thought of an all-powerful and loving God plotting to frustrate humanity by inventing an endless game of hide-and-seek was too outlandish for me to consider seriously. My outburst of laughter had been a necessary release of tension, but now I had to think this through and figure out what really made sense to me.

After a long time, my head cleared, and the following ideas began to take form and shape in my mind:

- If there is a God, it would have to be a supreme being, greater than anything that exists.

- For this being to be truly supreme, it would need to be the one creator of all life, encompassing the highest qualities we could ever imagine, such as unconditional love, pure wisdom, and omnipresence.

- As unconditional love, this being would cherish all creation and have compassion for all life.

- As pure wisdom, this being would create a variety of ethnicities, identities, and lifestyles, so that we could discover the rich diversity within unity.

- As omnipresent spirit, this being would exist in the soul of all life so that wherever we looked we would see the face of God.

Eventually I came to this conclusion:

- In order for God to *be* God, this supreme being must be the God of *all*.

I am not suggesting that these ideas came to me fully formed, but despite my young age I understood enough to provide myself with considerable comfort and a solid foundation from which I would later develop my personal philosophy. From that time on, I have never doubted the inclusive nature of Spirit.

As a student and teacher of world religions, I believe that God dwells in each soul, communicates in every language, celebrates all cultures, and loves all life equally. I also believe, as many sages have concluded, that all paths lead to God.

A Light in the Darkness

I chose to write about my first encounter with prejudice without emphasizing my religion of birth, because my story is by no means unique. The targeting and abuse of people because of the way they worship is a global dilemma that has plagued humanity for thousands of years.

My own experiences with prejudice and discrimination dominated my life for a long time. There were many occasions when I felt humiliated and demeaned by the words and actions of those who believed I was inferior and somehow evil.

In spite of everything, however, my repeated encounters with intolerance eventually served as a catalyst through which I became a stronger person. As time went on, I learned to stop thinking of myself as a victim and found ways to accept a newfound sense of personal dignity. With the help of wise teachers and counselors, I saw that it was not only possible for me to practice forgiveness but necessary that I do so in order to finally free myself from the anger and shame of the past.

During those years I also prayed fervently that one day I would find a way to help others embrace diversity and honor the presence of God in all people.

As an evolving peacemaker,

I walk the path of

courage.

Chapter 2

Searching for Truth

W hen I grew older, I traveled the world and became familiar with many cultures. I was fascinated by their religious practices and eventually majored in world religions in graduate school. While I enjoyed observing the unique ceremonies and rituals of the various sects, I was particularly interested in learning the similarities and differences among theologies.

After years of studying the holy books of a number of religious traditions, I concluded that the majority of the world's great religions were founded by those who possessed profound insights into the nature of humanity and were able to address the deepest needs of the human soul. They were master teachers, who taught by examples and parables designed to expand the intellect, touch the heart, and inspire hope for the future. Moreover, these leaders taught that it was possible for their followers to develop an inner connection with their deities that would provide a source of comfort for them in times of both joy and despair.

As I studied the various sacred scriptures, I found the following teachings common to all faiths:

- **Charity:** The act of providing for those less fortunate, benevolent giving, sharing freely of ourselves where it is needed

- **Compassion:** Loving our neighbors, living by the golden rule, sacrificing our needs for the well-being of others, reaching out in love

- **Forgiveness:** Letting go of grudges, making amends with those whom we have harmed or who have harmed us, shifting our thoughts from vengefulness to benevolence

- **Humility:** Modesty, graciousness, unpretentiousness, the absence of superiority

- **Praise:** Acts of gratitude, appreciation, thanksgiving, prayer, celebration

- **Peace:** The absence of war, nonviolence, living in harmony with others, inner contentment

- **Wisdom:** Understanding, insight, knowledge, discernment, justice

Also common to most theologies is the belief that people are capable of finding fulfillment through specific sacred disciplines, such as prayer, meditation, fasting, chanting, and other forms of devotion unique to their traditions.

There is another side to religion, however, that often seems to overshadow the timeless truths revealed by enlightened masters. Along with guidelines for living an ethical life and heartfelt verses flowing with gratitude and love, these same scriptures also contain historical accounts of violent wars, brutal torture, and mass murders—all seemingly sanctioned by God. The basis for these acts of violence are founded in the following theological concepts:

- **Exclusivity:** The belief that only one religion can be true, resulting in the divine command to exclude and destroy all enemies that practice false religions

- **The Angry Deity:** The idea that God is vengeful and punishes human imperfection. The belief that if one person transgresses the law the entire community must pay for the crime

- **Antagonistic Forces:** The belief that the world is divided by the forces of good and evil and that evil must be destroyed, thereby providing a moral justification for killing

These themes have become a breeding ground of violence for centuries, giving followers of different faiths permission to annihilate one another in an effort to follow God's will.

Of course, these scriptures were written hundreds of years ago. They speak to a time when verbal communication among nations was virtually nonexistent and various ethnic groups were constantly threatened with genocide. As I write these words, I realize that not much has changed over the years.

I am not suggesting that religion is the cause of violence. History shows that until modern times religion was intrinsically bonded with both politics and culture, making it difficult to know where one began and the other ended. Nevertheless, the threat of violence still hangs over our heads, and religion too often continues to divide rather than unite us.

This is why it is more important than ever to become familiar with the eternal wisdom that is present in all great religions. In this way we will see that, despite humanity's considerable differences, we are inextricably linked to one another through our deepest and most enduring mutual values, which are founded in love.

I have focused on violence among religions thus far, not only because it has been such an important part of my personal growth but because racial, cultural, and religious tensions make up such a large part of the terrorism that is running rampant in our world today. The catastrophic effects of prejudice and intolerance can be seen and felt on a daily basis.

What Does Our Future Hold?

How long do we expect to go on this way? Is it possible for humanity to exist indefinitely in a world overrun with wars, intolerance, and terrorism? Will our civilization that is steeped in centuries of violence eventually learn how to interact with others in more respectful and compassionate ways? We are running out of time, and unless we work at creating a new paradigm for living and find new ways to coexist, we will literally force ourselves into extinction. Can we make this enormous shift? Are we humans capable of actually lifting our consciousness from a culture of violence to a culture of peace?

Before we become overwhelmed by a sense of hopelessness, let us pause to consider the amazing ingenuity and inner resolve of the human spirit to accomplish things that have appeared to be impossible. From the great pyramids to walking on the moon to finding cures for diseases using advanced technology, humanity has proven, time and again, to possess an unwavering tenacity and a potential for greatness that goes beyond anything we could possibly imagine. No matter how hopeless the circumstances might seem, humanity has always prevailed and risen above adversity.

Yes, I believe the human race can and will make the necessary choices to create a safer, more compassionate world for our future generations. The blueprints for success exist in every soul and are written in every scripture. They have been voiced by great visionaries whose lives and teachings are powerful examples of how high humanity can soar when we choose to value the best in ourselves and others. One of the greatest of these visionaries is the legendary Mohandas Karamchand Gandhi (1869–1948), who was given the title of Mahatma, which means "Great Soul."

Mahatma Gandhi gifted the world with a timeless philosophy of nonviolence and in 1947 helped bring India to its independence, an achievement that was widely assumed to be impossible. Gandhi inspired other great teachers, such as Martin Luther King Jr., Nelson Mandela, and the Dalai Lama. Today, Gandhi's legacy lives on in the work of his grandson Arun Gandhi whose lectures and writings have helped keep the Gandhi vision alive and whose words have inspired me to put these ideas on paper.

Without a doubt, these are very challenging times, and there is a great deal of unrest in the world. People are being tortured and killed on a daily basis, and we are bombarded with conflicting points of view by political experts from one end of the spectrum to the other. There is cruelty and violence all around us. We are frightened for the future and helpless because we don't know how to make a difference in the world. It is time now to see that our only alternative lies in making a difference within ourselves.

> When I despair, I remember that all through history the way of truth and love have always won. There have been tyrants and murderers and for a time they can seem invincible, but in the end they always fall. Think of it ... always.[1]
>
> Gandhi

---

[1]   Mahatma Gandhi, *The Story of My Experiments with Truth* (Washington, Public Affairs Press, 1948)

As an evolving peacemaker,

I walk the path of

hope.

Chapter 3

One Person at a Time

A run Gandhi lectured at the Alex and Faye Spanos Theatre in San Luis Obispo, California in June of 2012 and his words made a life-altering impact on both me and my son, Matthew. As the fifth grandson of Mahatma Gandhi, Arun has devoted his life to sharing his grandfather's philosophy of nonviolence through his work as a writer, lecturer, teacher, and humanitarian.

I first became aware of Arun's work in 1998, when I did a phone interview with him for my radio program called *Positive Living*. He and his wife, Sunanda, had just written a fascinating biography of Arun's grandmother, called *The Forgotten Woman*, and he took time to discuss the book with me. I was deeply impressed with his presentation and wanted to learn more about the Gandhi teachings.

Later that year I invited Arun to come to Unity of San Luis Obispo, where I have served as minister since 1994, to facilitate a seminar for our community. The weekend was a great success, and Arun's insights touched the lives of all who attended.

by Leona Evans

Left to right: Sunanda Gandhi (1932–2007), Leona Evans, Matthew
J. Evans, and Arun Gandhi at Unity of San Luis Obispo, 1998

In the years following Arun's appearance at Unity, I often shared
his teaching stories with our congregation and hoped that when the
time was right he would one day speak again in San Luis Obispo.
That time came in June of 2012, when my wonderful son, Matthew,
was two months short of his sixteenth birthday.

Matthew J. Evans is a very talented young man who has been
a professional actor and musician since he was nine years old. He
started producing documentary short films at the age of twelve and
has won numerous awards at film festivals around the world.

As the child of a Unity minister, Matthew has always been very
comfortable with the New Thought teachings, which emphasize
inclusiveness and acceptance of all people. In addition, he has been
blessed with many opportunities to meet and make friends with those
of other cultures. These experiences, along with his early Montessori
education, offered Matthew wonderful opportunities to honor and
respect diversity among those of different faiths.

For a while Matthew assumed that everyone believed as he did,
but as he grew older and began to read historical accounts of wars
and violence among religions, his faith in humanity began to waver.

I sensed Matthew's deepening disappointment in the overall human condition and before long became aware of similar feelings stirring within myself.

The daily reports of terrorism and violence taking place throughout the world began to eat away at my faith in a future of peace. Little by little I felt less motivated to offer words of inspiration to Matthew or to my congregation. For the first time in years, I felt overwhelmed by the negativity around me and knew that my effectiveness as a minister would diminish significantly unless I chose to make some major changes in my own consciousness. I decided it was time for some words of wisdom from Arun Gandhi.

A Powerful Wake-Up Call

After checking his busy schedule, Arun agreed to do a speaking engagement in San Luis Obispo. Everyone at Unity looked forward to his appearance, including Matthew, who was too young to remember Arun's previous visit. Matthew really perked up when Arun gave him permission to make a documentary short film featuring Gandhi's views on the topic of nonviolence among religions. I had hope that as Matthew worked on the film his faith in the future of humanity, which had once given him such comfort, would be renewed. I also hoped the film would be an inspiration to other young people who were facing similar challenges.

Arun arrived in San Luis Obispo the day before his speaking engagement, and Unity hosted a buffet dinner in his honor. Arun has a gentle demeanor and a warm, engaging presence that draws people into his vibration. He was gracious enough to make time for all those who wished to speak with him. After a lovely dinner and stimulating conversation, I drove Arun to his hotel, and we agreed to meet early the next day to begin filming Matthew's documentary.

The following morning, we met Arun in his hotel suite. Matthew began setting up his film equipment, involving professional lights, three cameras, and a boom mike. I took the time to become familiar with the interview questions he had prepared for Arun. The plan was that Matthew would supervise the cameras and sound while I asked questions off-camera.

Arun Gandhi, *A Quest For Peace: Nonviolence Among Religions (2012)*

When everyone was ready, Matthew called, "Action!" and for the next two hours Arun gave wise and thought-provoking answers on the subject of nonviolence among religions. Then, just as the session drew to a close, Arun made a powerful statement that hit me like a jolt of electricity. He was speaking about the problems of war, when out of a deep sense of frustration, I interjected, "Our civilization has had such a long history of violence—how will humanity ever learn to live together in peace?" Arun looked at me for a moment and quietly replied, "One person at a time."

We took a break from filming, and I sat alone, thinking hard about the phrase "one person at a time." Why had it affected me so deeply? What did I need to learn from this? Why did those words seem like the missing piece of an all-important puzzle I hadn't been able to solve? After breathing deeply for a few moments I felt the pieces falling into place.

First I recalled a Gandhi teaching that described nonviolence as a pursuit rather than a possession, a way of life rather than the attainment of a goal. Slowly I began to grasp the meaning of Arun's comment. Like most people, I had learned to visualize peace as a destination rather than a journey and felt deeply frustrated because the world hadn't gotten there yet. I had been waiting impatiently for our world leaders to fix our international problems and make everyone stop fighting. More often than not, I'd been angry and discouraged that our leaders had not done their job. I thought the solution was in their hands and only they could make things better for us.

Then I started thinking about Arun Gandhi, traveling the world, planting seeds of peace, living the legacy of his grandfather, holding the belief that each of us can become the change we wish to see. In spite of major setbacks and tragedies along the way, his resolve has not wavered and his vision has not blurred. He is a peace activist devoting his life to the pursuit of nonviolence through speaking, teaching, and writing. In other words, Arun is *living* peace, not waiting for it.

My thoughts then shifted to the hundreds and thousands of people from all walks of life who, each day, reach out to one another in compassionate ways. They might not always make headlines, but if we look around we will see these everyday heroes sharing the best of themselves, paying it forward, promoting a culture of peace through single acts of kindness, and lifting the world with their love, one person at a time.

I decided not to waste any more time waiting for peace. Instead, I would learn to make peace with the journey itself and find ways to celebrate the small victories along the way.

Making Peace with the Process

I once took a leadership training course that emphasized the importance of process. The facilitator pointed out that when we create lofty and far-reaching visions for our future there is a tendency to feel overwhelmed if we find ourselves fixated on the distance between where we are and where we want to be. He suggested that we divide the bigger vision into a number of smaller, measurable goals. These goals should be reasonable and attainable, so that we learn to feel energized by our daily achievements instead of discouraged by the enormity of what lies before us.

Peace is a lifelong pursuit of truth, which begins inside of us and eventually touches the world. *Satyagraha* is the term Gandhi used to describe this state of mind. It is not a goal to reach but a way of life. We will study this important concept more deeply in the following chapters.

Arun's words "one person at a time" awakened my inner wisdom and opened the way for me to release my feelings of powerlessness. From then on I was free to become a conscious contributor to a culture of peace and to renew my commitment to this pursuit every day of my life. I realized that I would still be aware of the vast number of injustices that take place in our world, but I would no longer allow myself to feel defeated by them. After that day I chose to describe myself as an evolving peacemaker.

Later that afternoon, after the interview was over, Arun rested in his suite while I drove Matthew to the theater to set up three video cameras for the evening lecture. Matthew was thrilled to have spent quality time with Arun, and his eyes sparkled with excitement as he talked about how he would edit his upcoming documentary short film.

That evening, after Arun had spoken eloquently to an enthusiastic audience, he invited them to participate in a question-and-answer session. The questions from the audience reflected deep concerns about world issues, and Arun was able to acknowledge the seriousness of those problems while also conveying a sense of hope for the future. One of the most memorable questions came from a young college student who was feeling impatient because he could not seem to pound the concepts of nonviolence into the heads of some of his classmates who disagreed with him. Arun smiled at the notion of pounding peace into someone's head and replied that it is not by coercion but by example that genuine transformation takes place. He then shared one of the most powerful of all the Gandhi statements: "We must become the change we wish to see in the world."

Later that evening, after joining Arun and our guests for a late supper, Matthew and I drove home. We talked excitedly about our renewed faith in the future and shared some of our individual goals. We both agreed that we were entering a powerful period of new beginnings and vowed to practice more patience and compassion as we consciously embraced our lifelong journey as evolving peacemakers.

After a while, Matthew went up to bed and I relaxed on the sofa. As I reflected on the blessings we had experienced during the past few days, I was moved to offer a grateful prayer of thanks. Arun's visit had awakened a seed of hope within us. It was all that I had hoped for—and more.

The following morning, we took Arun to the airport and said our fond farewells as he departed San Luis Obispo and flew to another speaking engagement. Meanwhile, Matthew was excited to begin his work on an outline for his film. He had decided to add interviews with local leaders of other religious denominations to learn how they were promoting acceptance among religions.

As an evolving peacemaker,

I walk the path of

patience.

Chapter 4

A Quest for Peace

Over the next several weeks Matthew filmed interviews with a local Catholic priest, a Jewish rabbi, a Buddhist teacher, and a Muslim community leader as part of his documentary short film. The participants were very gracious with their time and gave us tours of their facilities. They were more than willing to become involved with the project. Each spiritual leader expressed great respect for the concept of nonviolence, and all were actively seeking ways to interact with those of other faiths in a spirit of acceptance and goodwill.

When the interviews were over, Matthew imported approximately five hundred minutes of footage into his computer. It took days to sort through all the interviews and make decisions about which footage to keep. Finally, it was time for Matthew to use his skills as a video editor and create a ten-minute film.

Matthew worked diligently on post-production, and after about two months of editing came up with a beautiful and uplifting piece of work called *A Quest For Peace: Nonviolence Among Religions.* The interviews in the film were tied together by Matthew's onscreen narration, which began as he expressed his growing concerns about the condition of our world.

Matthew stated, "I thought that if our political and religious leaders don't take action to put an end to violence and intolerance in our world, there might not be a world for my generation and no way humanity could ever live in peace. Then I met Arun Gandhi, who helped show me that one person can change the world."

Arun's contribution to the film was invaluable. His message focused on how important each individual is in helping to create a culture of peace through the practice of nonviolence. He emphasized that it is not about waiting for others to make the change; it is up to each one of us to *be* the change.

Matthew heard the message and internalized it. He ended the film on a note of hope. In the final scene, Matthew concluded, "Making this film has taught me that real change comes not by convincing others but by living the principles of nonviolence and being an example to others. If we do this, we can lift ourselves from the level of the problem to the level of the solution. I have hope that we will."

Arun was very pleased with the film and was eager to share it with his friends and colleagues. With Arun's blessing, I began submitting the work to local and international film festivals that had categories for youth filmmakers.

Arun and Matthew after a day of filming

The film festival market gives filmmakers of all ages and levels of expertise opportunities to have their work exhibited and evaluated by professionals as well as film audiences. The annual festivals, which are open to the public, can run anywhere from a weekend to a week. They also will host special events and activities throughout the year to celebrate the art of film. Being selected for a festival is an honor in itself, because so many films compete for just a few available slots on the program. Winning at these festivals is an even bigger honor, and occasionally scholarships or film editing software are awarded to student filmmakers in addition to plaques and certificates.

My primary goal in submitting *A Quest For Peace: Nonviolence Among Religions* to a large number of film festivals on Matthew's behalf was to share Arun Gandhi's words of wisdom with as many people as possible, thus introducing new ways of thinking to those not familiar with Gandhi's philosophy. I also wanted to support Matthew with opportunities to learn and grow as a filmmaker.

A Quest For Peace: Nonviolence Among Religions was an official selection at more than thirty festivals between 2012 and 2014. Matthew and I attended as many of these events as we could. At every Q&A after the screenings people would express their sincere admiration for the film. They were deeply impressed that a teenager would be so committed to the subject of nonviolence. Many were moved by the interfaith cooperation they witnessed in the film, which was something they had not seen before. Still others wanted to know more about the Gandhi teachings. They came away feeling new hope for the future. There were also those who sought our advice about the challenges that were tearing apart their own families as a result of religious intolerance. I counseled with some of them, and we agreed to stay in touch.

All in all, it was most gratifying to hear such positive feedback about the film and a tremendous blessing for Matthew to see that his efforts were inspiring people to look more deeply into the subject of nonviolence.

From 2012 through 2014, *A Quest For Peace: Nonviolence Among Religions* won top honors for Matthew as Best Youth Documentary

Filmmaker at nineteen film festivals throughout the United States. In addition, he was the only high school finalist in the 2013 Emerging Filmmakers Showcase at the Cannes Film Festival in France.

Matthew was also awarded a week-long scholarship to The FilmSchool's Prodigy Camp in Seattle in conjunction with the Seattle International Film Festival FutureWave competition. His time at camp afforded Matthew a tremendous opportunity to study and hone his technical and artistic skills as a filmmaker while connecting with peers who shared his passion for film.

In 2014, *A Quest For Peace* was a finalist for the Ron Kovic Peace Prize at the My Hero International Film Festival as well being a winner in their High School Documentary Film competition.

The most exciting honor of all, however, was still to come. One day in the spring of 2014, Matthew received a phone call from Carole Krechman, founder of The Peacemakers Corp, inviting him to accept a special award that would be presented to him at the United Nations' third High Level Forum on a Culture of Peace. Matthew will continue the story.

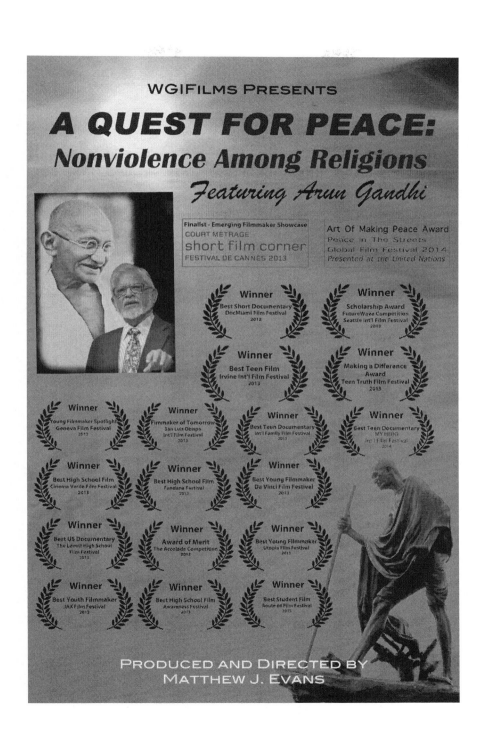

As an evolving peacemaker,

I walk the path of

creativity.

Chapter 5

An Invitation to the United Nations

by Matthew J. Evans

I was so excited to be going to the United Nations! I knew from the minute I heard I was to receive the Teen Art of Making Peace Award that it would be a life-changing experience. The award came from the Peace in the Streets Global Film Festival, which was organized by the PeaceMaker Corps, an NGO of the United Nations, which is headed by Carole Krechman. The mission of the Peacemaker Corps is to facilitate and support peace and tolerance among the youth of the world. The Peacemaker Corps empowers generations to come together and make our world a peaceful, compassionate, safe, and tolerant place to live.

When my Mom and I first saw the UN building, it felt as if we were walking towards Mount Olympus. I was awed and inspired by all the history that has been made there. This was where Eleanor Roosevelt organized the Universal Declaration of Human Rights from which the Culture of Peace is based. This is where nuclear weapon disarmament agreements have been reached to help protect the world from being destroyed by atomic bombs.

Looking up at the entrance to the United Nations, I saw an enormous sculpture created by Zurab Tsereteli, entitled *Good Defeats Evil,* which depicts St. George slaying a dragon; it is made from fragments of Soviet and US missiles. It was a gift to the UN from the Union of Soviet Socialist Republics after a large disarmament of nuclear weapons. The statue is at least thirty feet tall and is just amazing to see.

The day we were there, the main UN building was under renovation, so we didn't see the famous green-carpeted general assembly chamber. Instead, the High Level Forum was held in the UN Trusteeship Council Chamber, which was used as the general assembly hall while the main building was being renovated.

When I walked into the UN building and began soaking up the atmosphere, I experienced a tremendous feeling of awe. Everywhere I looked there was something interesting or exciting. There were portraits of all the former secretary generals, gifts to the UN from different nations (including a piece of the Berlin Wall), and meeting rooms everywhere filled with people discussing peace, education, trade, youth outreach, human rights, and everything else the UN supports. The biggest event of the day was the third High Level Forum on a Culture of Peace.

The High Level Forum was first organized in 2012, with ninety-seven member states participating. It has continued since then as an annual event, giving delegates the opportunity to reaffirm their commitment to peace and to speak about what they have done to improve the quality of life in their countries. We had the honor of attending both the morning and afternoon sessions.

Matthew and Leona in the UN Trusteeship Council Chamber

Before the morning session began, I got to meet the person who would present my award later that evening. His name is Ambassador Anwarul K. Chowdhury, and he has been president of the UN Security Council, president of the UNICEF Board, UN undersecretary general, senior special advisor to the UN General Assembly president, and permanent representative of Bangladesh. He has done amazing work during his career at the United Nations and has won high honors for his peacemaking efforts, including the U Thant Peace Award and the UNESCO Gandhi Gold Medal for Culture of Peace. I was very excited to receive my award from him!

The High Level Forum on a Culture of Peace was an incredible event. The huge meeting hall was filled with delegates and ambassadors representing countries from all over the world committed to making peace in some way. One of the things the Declaration on a Culture of Peace emphasizes is that peace isn't just the absence of military conflict but a continual process of improving education, the treatment of women, meeting environmental needs, solving the problems of hunger, ending discrimination, and so much more.

by Leona Evans

I've never seen so many people from around the world gathered in one location for such a high purpose. It was so inspiring to me. Not only is it incredible that each nation is participating in some way toward the development of peace, but collectively we're working toward a shared goal. This is the greatest example of the peacemaking process. If different countries from around the world can share ideas on creating a peaceful world, what's to stop us from sitting down and peacefully sharing our ideas at home? In our neighborhoods? In our schools?

Origin of the United Nations

The UN began as the League of Nations on January 10, 1920 and was a dream of President Woodrow Wilson to establish an international organization focused on maintaining peace in the world. However, because of political unrest within the United States and other parts of the world, the League never really got off the ground. The assistant secretary of the Navy at that time, Franklin D. Roosevelt, believed in the idea of an international peacekeeping force and had the vision to continue that goal.

At the end of World War II, fifty-one countries, including the United States, the United Kingdom, China, the Soviet Union, Australia, Poland, Denmark, and India, all came together to form the United Nations, headquartered in New York City.

One thing I realized in my time at the UN was how little I actually knew about it. Sometimes I hear people ask, "What does the UN do?" The truth is that billions of dollars have been put into programs that help prevent violence against minorities, vaccinate those in disease-ridden areas, and provide food, water, and education where needed.

Organizations within the UN

UNICEF is the United Nations International Children's Emergency Relief Fund. It won the Nobel Peace Prize for its work in helping children around the world. In 2015, UNICEF responded to 310 humanitarian situations in over one hundred countries. They

- gave 127,000 people in Haiti access to clean water;

- helped provide 908,000 Syrian children in refugee camps throughout the Middle East with a formal education;

- assisted 3.7 million people in Africa during the ebola crisis by teaching them about prevention and protection from ebola;

- gave 334,000 children in Burundi the measles vaccine, helping the world get closer to eradicating that disease;

- provided 1.6 million people in Ukraine access to safe water in the midst of the conflict involving Russia and the Ukraine;

- saved over 160,000 children in Afghanistan under the age of six from severe acute malnutrition (SAM);

- liberated 146 children in Myanmar from armed forces and provided them with proper medical treatment, job training, education, and financial aid; and

- provided 41,584 households in the Central African Republic with plumbing for sanitation and drinking purposes.

For a complete list of all of UNICEF's accomplishments and activities, I recommend reading their Annual Results Report Humanitarian Action at (www.unicef.org/about).

The Food and Agriculture Organization (FAO) has distributed quality seeds to independent farmers in Haiti to help lower food prices and feed the nation's people. Just recently they partnered with the Global Soil Partnership to do a study examining topsoil erosion in Malawi and produced new guidelines for more sustainable and effective farming in some of the most impoverished areas in the world.

The University for Peace based in Costa Rica is the only academic organization in the world that offers graduate degrees with specific courses designed to promote peace, such as Responsible Management, Sustainable Development, Media, Peace and Conflict Studies, and many others.

The Human Settlements Programme (UN-Habitat) works on ensuring sustainable urban development and upgrading conditions in our towns and cities. The program is focused on seeing that highly concentrated urban areas have access to clean water. In Haiti, they assisted with disaster relief and reconstruction. In the Democratic Republic of the Congo, they provide programs to fight slum growth and alleviate housing problems. They work in over seventy countries and have made major contributions to better living situations all over the world.

UN Women is a program to actively track international progress for women's rights. This database is full of various markers of progress and examines every nation's constitution to see what protections women have and what is needed.

UNESCO stands for the United Nations Educational, Scientific and Cultural Organization. Their mission is to promote better relationships with people around the world through the exchange of ideas.

Part of UNESCO is the Global Alliance for Cultural Diversity. They hold annual worldwide events, such as International Jazz Day, International Literacy Day, International Day of Peace, Migrants Day, World Environment Day, International Day of the World's Indigenous People, and dozens of other events to honor cultural diversity.

The UNHCR, or the UN Refugee Agency, is dedicated to helping and protecting refugees. They work to help those in need to safely leave their troubled homelands and find shelter around the world. In recent months, they've been working in Syria, Turkey, and Mozambique to help the massive relocations there.

The International Labor Organization (ILO) focuses on improving labor conditions around the world, helping to create fair wages and ending modern-day slavery. Some of their recent accomplishments include establishing vocational training for underprivileged people in Bangladesh, exposing unsafe working conditions for health-care workers in China, and a Child Support Grant for children in South Africa, which has given money to help over 11 million children living in poverty.

The UNIDO is the Industrial Development organization. Its mission is to help developing nations establish their own industries. They work with member nations to share their resources, expertise, and knowledge with less developed countries.

Recently UNIDO partnered with South Korea to host an industrial policy training course. The goal of the course was to share inclusive and sustainable policies for running factories and research institutions.

The peacekeeping forces of the UN are those who wear the famous blue helmets and put their lives on the line to protect people in the midst of conflict. The approximately 111,000 peacekeepers have been deployed all over the world, protecting civilians during civil wars, revolutions, and uprisings. The peacekeeping forces have a permanent place in Africa to protect its citizens.

Critical Observations

As in any worldwide organization with high-minded ideas, there will always be times that goals are not met. Some of the biggest criticisms toward the United Nations have been in relation to their failure to prevent several of the most violent genocides in recent years. Some say that the genocides in Rwanda and Bosnia could have been stopped by the UN peacekeeping forces, but they either reacted too slowly or failed to react at all.

Another major criticism of the UN is the veto power of the Security Council. The five permanent members of the Security Council (the United States, Russia, China, France, and the United Kingdom) all have veto power. This veto power can be used on any resolution put forth in the Security Council, even with majority support. This means that if one out of the five permanent members on the council rejects a plan, it's completely dead. One example of this is Russia and China's veto of UN intervention in the Syrian civil war, in which thousands of innocent civilians have been killed.

These failures are devastating and shouldn't be discounted, but I believe overall the UN is making great contributions throughout the world. Their ineffective or harmful actions in some instances shouldn't negate the beneficial and necessary work that is done by the UN.

Aside from the major bodies of the UN that I mentioned earlier, there are over fourteen hundred nongovernmental organizations (NGOs) specifically associated with the UN that do a lot of good work. In fact, NGOs are specifically designed to be nonprofit organizations that focus on humanitarian action. They aren't involved with any military forces and are ideally unbiased and solely committed to helping others throughout the world.

Sometimes NGOs have been criticized for showing too much bias towards one side or another. However, despite the criticism, it's clear that nongovernmental organizations do a tremendous amount of important work. I highly recommend participating in specific organizations that speak to your interests and passions.

I felt a deep sense of global community at the UN. The employees who greeted us seemed to be as internationally diverse as the flags. Everywhere we looked we saw different styles of clothing and heard different dialects and languages. People were smiling, and it felt like living in a world of peace.

The Art of Making Peace Award

The awards ceremony for the Peace in the Streets Global Film Festival was really special. All of the winning short films were shown, and then came time for the awards presentation. My film was the finale of the night, and Ambassador Chowdhury introduced my award, which was called the Teen Art of Making Peace Award. Here is what he said:

> For all young people who have come here to the UN on the occasion of the third High Level Forum on a Culture of Peace, this is a very special occasion. For you, for all of us. Months of work and finally we are ending this day with this wonderful ceremony and award presentation. If you provide young people a voice, a platform, or a medium like filmmaking, you have made a contribution to the culture of peace. I think this is very important. It's wonderful that you have chosen to take the medium of filmmaking for promoting peace. Films can be made to bring peace and end violence in the streets but at the same time I see and believe that this phrase *peace in the streets* also means that peace is something very simple. It can be brought about by anybody at any level, and it has its contribution to a broader global movement for the culture of peace.

> So I would now like to read the award. The first annual Peacemaker Corps Peace in the Streets Global Film Festival. This is the highest award given to Matthew J. Evans of Santa Maria, California. And the title of his film is *A Quest For Peace: Nonviolence Among Religions,* September 9, 2014, United Nations, New York.

At this point I came onstage, and Ambassador Chowdhury gave me a very warm handshake and did his best to put the medal around my neck without also taking off my glasses in the process. After presenting the award he said,

> "I must say congratulations. Your film which we saw here and I saw earlier also is wonderful. This is a very powerful message. You are a good filmmaker!"

Ambassador Chowdhury and Matthew

Receiving praise like that from such an important global ambassador for peace was truly an honor. I felt validated as a peacemaker-filmmaker and inspired to continue working towards creating a culture of peace such as the UN is helping to establish every day.

It was ironic that during the High Level Forum on the Culture of Peace, literally during the exact same time, the Security Council was called to a meeting, most likely to discuss how to deal with the early threat of ISIS (the Islamic State of Iraq and the Levant, also known as the Islamic State of Iraq and Syria). At the time, the Islamic State hadn't become the huge organization it is today, but still knowing that the Security Council was discussing the air strikes, militias, and strategies that would make headlines in the subsequent months was unnerving. In one room people from around the world were pledging their commitment to peace, while just down the hall people from the same countries were deciding issues of life and death.

At different times, I feel confused about that situation. Sometimes I feel cynical. Is it hypocritical to be talking about making peace among nations, cultures, and religions when on the same day you're organizing drone strikes on an enemy force? Can violence ever really bring about peace?

Other times I feel more optimistic. I hear a really inspiring speech and I think, *Oh my gosh—everyone is going to put down their weapons tomorrow and we'll have world peace* right now! Of course that's an unreasonable expectation, and I have to keep remembering that.

In our interview for *A Quest For Peace*, Arun said that peace could only happen one person at a time. It's not turning everything around in a single day. The mission should be to reach out to one single person and treat that person with respect, love, and compassion every day of our lives. When we do this, we plant a seed for peace. It might not grow right away. The person might still be guided by hate and prejudice, but it also might grow and inspire someone else to look at the world in a different way.

If we plant many seeds and reach out to everyone without discrimination, we will begin to build bridges in our communities, which will slowly spread and affect others far beyond our own circle of friends, family, and co-workers. The process might seem overwhelming, but after meeting with Arun and going to the UN, where so many people are dedicating their lives to creating a culture of peace, I want to do everything I can to help make it happen!

Reflections

Matthew's United Nations experience inspired him to become a citizen of the world. He witnessed representatives from many countries dedicating their lives to the support of peace, sustainable development, and human rights, each in their own unique way. It was then and there that Matthew decided to become part of this worldwide movement through his work as a filmmaker, actor, and musician.

My own creative journey involves completing and publishing *The Evolving Peacemaker*. I then plan on continuing to support Matthew with his creative projects and devoting my time to promoting a culture of peace through films, books, television, classes, Sunday services, seminars, social media, and interfaith events.

As an evolving peacemaker,

I walk the path of

global awareness.

My grandfather believed that truth should be the cornerstone of everybody's life and that we must dedicate our lives to pursuing truth, to finding out the truth in our lives. And so his entire philosophy was the philosophy of life. It was not just a philosophy for conflict resolution but something we have to imbibe in our life and live all the time so that we can become better human beings. We can never overcome violence with more violence. We can only overcome violence with respect, understanding and love for each other.[2]

Arun Gandhi

---

[2] "Satyagraha 100 Years Later: Gandhi Launches Modern Non-Violent Resistance Movement on Sept. 11, 1906," published 10/6/2006 <u>democracynow. org/2006/9/8/satyagraha 100 years later gandhi launches</u>

Chapter 6

Satyagraha: A Philosophy of Nonviolence

T he concept of satyagraha (sat-**ya**-graha) is the foundation of the Gandhi philosophy of nonviolence. It is a multifaceted term that can be interpreted as the lifelong and active pursuit of truth. Satyagraha is the process through which we strive to meet violence with nonviolence every day of our lives. Gandhi stated, "Satyagraha is a relentless search for truth and a determination to teach truth through nonviolent means."[3]

Satyagraha embodies the ideas of conflict resolution through nonviolent action, respect, and ethical behavior. It is also a philosophy of living that embraces inclusiveness, compassion, strength of purpose, personal discipline, and faith.

---

[3]   Gandhi, Young India, May 7, 1919

by Leona Evans

Mohandas Karamchand Gandhi (1869–1948)

Arun shares this story:

> When my grandfather Mohandas Karamchand Gandhi developed his philosophy of nonviolence in South Africa and wanted an appropriate word to describe it, he could not find one. He rejected "passive resistance" and "civil disobedience" saying there was nothing passive or disobedient about the movement. He even offered a reward to anyone who could come up with a positive English word to describe what he had in mind. Alas, no one could.
>
> Gandhi decided a Sanskrit word might be more appropriate, as he was planning to move back to India and lead the Indian struggle for freedom. He found *satyagraha*, a combination of two Sanskrit words, described his philosophy the best: *satya* meaning "truth," and *agraha* meaning "the pursuit of." Thus satyagraha means the pursuit of truth, the opposite of the Western concept of possessing the truth. Nonviolence, therefore, can be described as an honest and diligent pursuit

of truth. Nonviolence can also mean the search for the meaning of life or the purpose of life.[4]

Satyagraha can be understood as a spiritual philosophy that has its foundation in the inherent goodness of humanity and our continual quest for peace.

The Grain of Wheat

Arun's grandfather liked to tell a favorite story about an ancient Indian king who insisted on finding the meaning of peace. As he searched for answers throughout his kingdom he would ask, "What is peace? How can we get it? What should we do when we find it?"

After a time, the king found an old man who had the reputation of being very wise. When the king asked, "What is peace?" the sage simply handed him a single grain of wheat. The king was puzzled but did not want to admit his ignorance. Instead, he took the grain and put it in a small gold box for safekeeping. Each morning the king would open the tiny box and study the grain, hoping somehow to find enlightenment, but he found nothing. Eventually another sage passed through town, and the king eagerly sought him out to solve his dilemma.

"'It is quite simple, your honor,' said the sage. 'Just as this grain represents nourishment for the body, peace represents nourishment for the soul. Now if you keep this grain locked up in a gold box it will eventually perish without providing nourishment or multiplying. However, if it is allowed to interact with the elements of light, water, air, and soil it will flourish and multiply and soon you would have a whole field of wheat to nourish not only you but so many others. This is

---

[4] "Arun Gandhi Reflects on Working Toward Peace, Santa Clara University, accessed July 12, 2016, legacy.scu.edu/ethics/architects-of-peace/Gandhi/essay.html

the meaning of peace. It must nurture your soul and the souls of others.'"[5]

This allegory teaches that peace is not a tangible thing that we can find and keep for ourselves. The king represents the part of our ego that believes peace is a private treasure which we can experience only by shutting ourselves off from everyday life and the emotional challenges of relating to others. "Don't disturb my peace of mind," we are likely to tell our family and friends—as though peace is something fragile and must be carefully hidden or it will dissipate. In fact, the opposite is true.

The grain of wheat symbolizes the seed of peace, which is already within us. When we keep it hidden, it remains a mystery to us and eventually withers from lack of use. However, as we plant our seed by extending compassion to others and staying true to the principles of nonviolence, those attributes multiply.

Each seed planted in the name of love and truth provides spiritual nourishment for us and those around us. We cultivate our inherent ability to feel stronger and more connected to all of life. We develop greater patience and faith in humanity. We let go of the distinctions between *them* and *us* and become willing to embrace the greatest of our spiritual gifts—the capacity to see ourselves in others.

Does reaching out to the world mean we should not take time for ourselves? Not at all. Daily times of quiet meditation nourish the soul and provide us with much needed times of relaxation, revitalization, and an opportunity to feel a connection with the spirit of God within us. Regular times of meditation also remind us of our commitment to continue planting seeds of peace, by extending to others the same level of compassion we wish for ourselves. This is how the seeds begin to grow and multiply.

---

[5]   Ibid

Satyagraha and Social Justice

There is another component involved in the concept of satyagraha that describes Gandhi's particular form of nonviolence through social action and the reasons behind it. He stated, "Satyagraha is soul force, pure and simple."[6]

Gandhi wanted people to be clear about the difference between passive resistance and nonviolent resistance, because he felt the word "passive" had a connotation of weakness that caused some to think he supported nonaction in the face of injustice. This is definitely not the case. Gandhi's philosophy of nonviolence is not based in weakness or nonaction but in the invincible power of love, which gives people the courage to stand strong in the face of persecution and oppression without resorting to physical violence. He encouraged people to take a nonviolent stand against anything that would demean or oppress humanity. He was not against taking action, only the use of physical force.

Gandhi set very high standards for those who would practice satyagraha in relation to nonviolent resistance:

- They must be grounded in love and have the utmost respect for the law, so that when they chose not to cooperate with specific legislation others could acknowledge the importance of their concern.

- The act of nonviolent resistance was reserved for an unjust law that severely diminished the quality of life and human dignity. It was not to be used randomly.

- Gandhi ruled out the destruction of property, foul language, physically trying to block people, or any type of bullying or intimidation.

---

[6]   Satyagraha in South Africa, Nayahivan, Ahmedabad, 1928 pp 109–115

- For Gandhi civil disobedience focused on the *civil* way it was to be conducted. Gandhi believed that by demonstrating love and a willingness to take on legal penalties, they would eventually move the authorities to experience a change of heart and become willing to negotiate.

The work began in September of 1906. Gandhi spoke before three thousand Indians gathered in a theater in Johannesburg, South Africa. There he organized a strategy of satyagraha designed to oppose the racist policies which were in place there. He explained that the purpose of satyagraha was to reveal truth and confront injustice with nonviolence. This process often involved acts of great physical stamina and a willingness to make personal sacrifices for the greater good.

The satyagraha movement in South Africa grew to such an extent that by 1913 thousands of Indians were refusing to cooperate with laws they felt were demeaning and inhumane. The jails were overcrowded, and local as well as international press were writing articles about Gandhi's philosophy of nonviolence. Finally, Gandhi was called to deliberate with government officials to repeal some of the harsh treatment of Indians. Those deliberations resulted in the Indian Relief Act of 1914, which included recognizing Indian marriages, abolishing an existing poll tax, and relaxing immigration laws.

While many issues of discrimination were not addressed in the Indian Relief Act, the repeal of some of the harsher laws was regarded as a tremendous victory. When Gandhi returned to India he was greeted with the name *Mahatma*, which means "great soul."

Gandhi's work was a great inspiration to Nelson Mandela. At the unveiling of the Gandhi memorial statue in Pietermaritzburg, South Africa, on June 6, 1993, Dr. Mandela stated:

Gandhiji influenced the activities of liberation movements, civil rights movements, and religious organizations in five continents of the world. He impacted on men and women who have achieved significant historical changes in their countries not least amongst whom is Martin Luther King.

The Mahatma is an integral part of our history because it is here that he first experimented with truth; here that he demonstrated his characteristic firmness in pursuit of justice, here that he developed satyagraha as a philosophy and a method of struggle.

Perhaps Gandhi's most legendary demonstration of satyagraha was the Salt March of 1930 in India. During the time of British rule, one of the many injustices Britain imposed on India was a law that forbade Indians from manufacturing or selling their own salt. They were forced to import salt from Britain at a very high price, which was a hardship to the many who could not afford it. Since salt was a nutritional necessity in India, where the climate is often hot and humid, Gandhi saw this law as inexcusable.

When the Indian National Congress met in January of 1930, they agreed to intensify their efforts toward independence. At that time many expected Gandhi to launch a high-profile satyagraha campaign. Instead he chose to center the campaign around the salt issue. Those close to him were surprised that instead of choosing one of the more pressing injustices Gandhi chose to focus on the simple issue of salt. However, for Gandhi this was a clear example of how invasive Britain's control was on the most basic aspects of Indian life.

On March 2, 1930, Gandhi wrote a letter to British Viceroy Lord Irwin asking for a number of repeals, including a repeal of the salt tax. He informed Irwin that if his letter was ignored he would launch a satyagraha campaign. Irwin did not reply, and Gandhi went ahead with his plans.

At dawn on March 12, 1930, Gandhi and several dozen companions began a 241-mile walk from his ashram near Ahmedabad to the Arabian Sea town of Dandi. It was Gandhi's goal to harvest salt from the beachside as a symbolic statement of freedom from oppression.

On the way Gandhi stopped at dozens of villages and gave speeches denouncing the salt tax. In a matter of days, thousands of Indians joined the march. Journalists from the *New York Times* and other newspapers began following the journey as well.

When they arrived at their destination and Gandhi performed the illegal act of picking up a small piece of salt-filled mud from the shore, the Salt Satyagraha officially began, and Gandhi was arrested. In the following weeks, supporters came to the seaside in droves to harvest salt. During that time approximately eighty thousand people were arrested, and many were assaulted by the police. Journalists witnessed hundreds of marchers being beaten over the head and not a single one raising an arm to strike back. Stories of these events circulated widely in the international media, causing great sympathy for India and much humiliation for Britain.

When Gandhi was released from prison in early 1931 he was more revered than ever. *Time Magazine* honored him as its 1930 Man of the Year and British Viceroy Lord Irwin agreed to negotiate with him. The talks resulted in the Gandhi-Irwin Pact, which gave Indians living by the sea the right to harvest salt and included the release of thousands of political prisoners.

Gandhi and his followers continued practicing satyagraha for the next sixteen years, until India was finally granted its independence in 1947. Gandhi's idealism, perseverance, and complete dedication to the philosophy of nonviolence have been a shining example of the greatness humanity can achieve when motivated by truth and love.

The Reverend Martin Luther King Jr. wrote about Gandhi's influence on his own life and work:

> The whole concept of Satyagraha ... was profoundly significant to me. As I delved deeper into the philosophy of Gandhi my skepticism concerning the power of love gradually diminished, and I came to see for the first time its potency in the area of social reform ... Love for Gandhi was a potent instrument for social and collective transformation. It was in this Gandhian emphasis on love and nonviolence

that I discovered the method for social reform that I had been seeking for so many months ... I came to feel that this was the only morally and practically sound method open to oppressed people in their struggle for freedom.[7]

Gandhi believed that an important way to understand the nature of nonviolence was to learn some key ideas about the nature of violence. He understood that there are various components of violence that involve more than physical force. Sometimes they are so subtle we might not even recognize them. Nevertheless, the more we learn about the many ways violence can occur the more prepared we will be to identify some of our own issues and set about the process of healing them.

For Gandhi, violence had both a physical and nonphysical form. He believed that just because we refrain from using physical violence doesn't mean we are not wounding others with our words. Words can serve as lethal weapons and produce harmful results whether we mean them to or not. Gandhi referred to nonphysical violence as passive violence, which has the potential to do much harm if left unacknowledged and untreated.

---

[7] King, "Stride Toward Freedom: The Montgomery Story" Boston, MA, Beacon Press; Reprint edition (January, 2010)

As an evolving peacemaker,

I walk the path of

nonviolent action.

Grandfather asked me to build a genealogical tree of violence with "physical" and "passive" as the two branches. Every night he would help me analyze my day's experiences and put them down on the tree. Passive violence was where physical violence was not employed. In a few months I filled up one wall in my room with acts of passive violence and the experience has remained with me ever since.[8]

Arun Gandhi

[8] "One God, Many Images By Arun Gandhi," The Network of Spiritual Progressives, accessed July 12, 2016
spiritualprogressives.org/newsite/?p=653

Chapter 7

The Many Faces of Passive Violence

You would be surprised to know how much violence each one of us commits in spite of the fact that we don't go out and fight.[9]

Arun Gandhi

Gandhi emphasized that in order to fully grasp his philosophy of nonviolence we first had to admit that consciously or unconsciously we engage in a certain type of violence every day of our lives. He referred to this behavior as passive violence. Gandhi taught that violence has two forms: physical and passive. The first form of violence is much more obvious because it involves physical force. Many of us think of violence only in its physical form and will often say, "I don't participate in violent behavior, because I communicate with my words instead of my fists." However, there are many words in our vocabulary that represent something quite demeaning, such as name-calling, teasing, and putting others down. The practice of these can have a direct connection to physical violence, as Arun points out:

The relationship between passive violence and physical violence is the same as the relationship between gasoline and

---

[9]   Gandhi shares his grandfather's message of nonviolence, Shan't Shahrigian, *The Riverdale Press*, posted September 25, 2013 (riverdalepress.com/stories/Gandhi-shares-his-grandfathers-message-of-nonviolence,53016)

fire. Acts of passive violence generate anger in the victim, and since the victim has not learned how to use anger positively, the victim abuses anger and generates physical violence. Thus it is passive violence that fuels the flame of physical violence, which means that if we wish to put out the fire of physical violence we have to cut off the fuel supply.[10]

How often does passive violence lead to physical violence? Look at the number of schoolchildren who commit violent crimes against themselves and others after being teased and bullied. Think of the physical altercations that take place during public events because of name-calling and hateful slurs. I'm sure the vast majority of us can recall times when we have been so deeply offended by the words of others that we were tempted to lash out physically in retaliation. Perhaps at times we reacted so strongly that we actually did lash out. The key word here is *react*.

Too often we allow others to affect us so deeply with their words that we lose emotional and sometimes physical control of our responses. Then we feel compelled to defend ourselves with the familiar clichés: "I couldn't help it." "They made me do it." "I didn't have a choice." We convince ourselves that we can't control our own behavior until others change their ways. Arun explains:

> Unless we change individually, no one is going to change collectively. For generations we have been waiting for the other person to change first. A change of heart cannot be legislated; it must come out of conviction.[11]

One of our goals as evolving peacemakers is to carefully observe the words we use in our daily interactions with others. As we learn

---

[10] Matthew J. Evans, *A Quest For Peace: Nonviolence Among Religions* (WGIFilms, 2012)

[11] "Arun Gandhi: "In Pursuit" of Peace," Marilyn Turkovich, Voices Compassion Education, posted March 21, 2012 voiceseducation.org/content/arun-gandhi-pursuit-peace)

more about the many voices of passive violence, we will see that they run the gamut from the volatile use of obscenities and verbal bullying to the so-called harmless joke and the quietest and most subtle forms of sarcasm. The more aware we are of the power of our words, the more responsible we can be for the ways we use them.

Passive Violence and Bullying

If we want to teach real peace in this world we should start by educating children.[12]

Gandhi

Those of us who are parents want to protect our children and keep them safe from harm. However, we realize we can't always protect them, because an important part of growing up involves learning to cope effectively with conflicts and the daily challenges of life. Our children will undoubtedly have altercations with their peers and in many cases learn valuable lessons from those experiences without excessive interference from parents or teachers. However, if our children are being bullied with hateful slurs and vicious name-calling, they have become victims of passive violence and need every ounce of our support to help heal the situation through nonviolent action.

The website stopbullying.gov is managed by the US Department of Health and Human services and is designed to help parents, teachers, family members, and friends of school-aged children understand more about bullying. It also provides resources to help people find ways to respond effectively to this devastating problem. They define bullying in the following way:

---

[12] Mahatma Gandhi, *Collected Work of Mahatma Gandhi*, GandhiServe Foundation, 2003 Vol. 54, pg 98–100

Bullying is unwanted, aggressive behavior among school-aged children that involves a real or perceived power imbalance. The behavior is repeated, or has the potential to be repeated over time. Bullying includes actions such as making threats, spreading rumors, attacking someone physically or verbally, and excluding someone from a group on purpose.

Verbal bullying includes repeated threats, name-calling, teasing, inappropriate sexual comments, and any form of degrading remarks based on a child or teen's appearance, race, disabilities, mental capacities, or sexual orientation. Social bullying involves spreading false rumors, intentionally ostracizing certain children from group activities, or repeatedly shaming them in front of their peers. Cyberbullying involves using the Internet, email, texting, and other forms of digital technologies for the purpose of humiliating and diminishing those who are the targets.

Bullies generally focus on those who are perceived as different and who are often regarded as unpopular, introverted, and unable to defend themselves. Bullying can happen anywhere and at any time. Children and teens who are regular victims of bullying can often suffer serious emotional scarring, which can lead to self-esteem problems, depression, and even suicide.

It is most important for parents and teachers to discuss the facts of bullying with their children or students and help them understand that nobody deserves to be bullied. Holding seminars at schools and promoting the use of nonviolent actions are powerful ways to help put an end to this insidious form of passive violence. No one should have to go through this kind of abuse alone.

In addition to addressing and learning about bullying, we need to become aware of warning signs that might alert us to negative changes in our child's behavior. We must have a strong and loving support system in place to help the family understand and cope with these changes. Most importantly, we need to let our children know that we are there for them and will do our best to support them any way we can.

Some of these ways include talking with our child's teachers, discussing the issue with other parents, seeking support from groups comprised of child advocates and peer support networks, monitoring our child's use of social media, and providing our child with professional counseling services. The more attention and professional expertise we bring to the issue of bullying the more effective we will be in contributing to positive changes in our environment.

What about the Bullies?

An issue we often overlook involves the bullies themselves. What problems must they be suffering in order to behave so despicably to those who are smaller or weaker than they? Have they been abused? Do they have a distorted sense of themselves? Have they had tragic home lives and need to feel in control of their environment? Do they have emotional problems that could be treated by a professional therapist?

No matter how many difficulties these young people might be suffering, there is never an excuse for bullying. There are, however, steps that can be taken to place bullies in a loving and therapeutic environment designed to heal the wounds of their past and help them learn a more effective way of interacting with their peers.

Perhaps some of you who are reading these words right now might wish to help solve this devastating problem. Whether you are a social worker, spiritual advisor, teacher, parent, doctor, nurse, or attorney, please consider contacting a group in your area that is willing to extend compassion and professional expertise to those young people who feel compelled to express their pain and rage by bullying others.

If we do not take positive, nonviolent action, there is every possibility these bullies will one day end up in prison with little to no chance of receiving the rehabilitation they so desperately need. The way to heal violence is not by adding more violence but by meeting it with love and wisdom.

Other Forms of Passive Violence

Passive violence takes many forms and occurs in varying degrees, sometimes so subtly that we barely recognize it for what it is. Examples of passive violence can include sarcastic humor, gossip, insults, and inappropriate references to one's ethnicity, lifestyle, or appearance. These remarks can be made about us or by us. They can be spoken with rage, mild irritation, or sometimes with a smile, which can leave invisible but indelible emotional scars.

While we cannot be expected to take responsibility for peoples' reactions to what we say, we must always be responsible for what we actually *mean* when we say it. It is not only the words we speak but the attitude behind our words that give them power.

For example, we can make an effort to communicate clearly with our words. However, if we have unresolved feelings about the subject matter or the person with whom we are conversing, our real feelings will affect our tone of voice, and we will inadvertently send out a mixed message. "I have no problem with that," or, "I'm sorry you feel that way," are examples of words that can convey a very different meaning depending upon our vocal inflections and body language. These nuances are not always obvious to us, but the other person can often sense when there is some anger behind our words. This is why it is not unusual to hear people comment, "It's not what you said but the way you said it that hurt my feelings."

As evolving peacemakers, we need to remember that we are responsible for finding and healing any inner resentments that might be lurking behind our words. In this way we can stay true to ourselves and communicate more effectively and compassionately with others.

Self-Condemnation as Passive Violence

It might come as a shock to discover that even if we stayed away from those who would use their words against us we would still be left with the negative judgments we inflict upon ourselves.

How often do we use passive violence against ourselves? Let us begin by asking some important questions: "How often do I put myself down?" "How frequently do I berate myself for past mistakes and end up losing confidence in my own abilities?" "How harshly do I judge myself for not living up to my own expectations or those of others?"

Committing passive violence against ourselves has devastating effects not only on our emotional well-being but on our relationships as well. A major step toward self-acceptance and anger management begins by agreeing to uplift the content of our self-talk.

Too often we commit passive violence by calling ourselves names. "Wow, am I stupid!" "What an idiot I am!" "How fat (skinny, ugly, ineffective) I am."

Frequently we find ourselves criticizing our past behaviors by replaying old conversations in our mind. "I should have said this." "Why didn't I say that?" "How could I have let this happen?" "I should have kept my big mouth shut." "Why didn't I speak up?"

Most people engage in negative self-talk on a regular basis and don't even give it a second thought. Oddly enough, when others refer to us in similar ways we react with hurt and anger. "How can they be so insensitive?" we ask, not realizing that the words they used are similar to the ones we use against ourselves. Too often we are overly sensitive to those criticisms from others because of our underlying fears that what they have said about us might be true.

I remember years ago when I first became aware of how frequently and unconsciously I used passive violence against myself. One of my friends had come over and found me frantically searching the contents of my trash can for an item I had mistakenly thrown away. Watching me and shaking her head, she casually referred to me as stupid. I immediately became defensive and sharply replied, "How can you be so rude? How dare you speak to me that way!"

My friend registered confusion and irritation at my sudden burst of anger. "What's the big deal?" she asked indignantly. "You call yourself stupid all the time!"

It took me a moment to realize she was right. I often described myself in pejorative terms, usually as a response to uncomfortable or embarrassing situations. I would say to friends or family, "What a stupid thing I just did" or "I sure hope I don't act stupid at the party like I did last time."

During that period of my life I figured that if I mentioned my mistakes before anyone else did I wouldn't look so foolish. I was a perfectionist and tried really hard to avoid making mistakes, especially in front of others.

Suddenly that word *stupid* was coming at me from another person, and I was deeply offended. The ensuing argument ended up putting a strain on our relationship for several months.

Sadly, I came to see that even if my friend never again called me stupid it was likely that I would still use that term or something like it to berate myself. This was a major turning point for me, and I finally admitted that even though the bullies of my childhood were long gone, a part of me still feared that what they had once thought of me was true.

Without realizing it, I had become my own bully by replacing their voices with my own and perpetuating the cycle of passive violence. I saw in that moment how important it was to find ways to unite the warring factions inside of me and make peace with the passive violence within myself.

As an evolving peacemaker,

I walk the path of

self-discovery.

It is the duty of every human being to look carefully within and see himself as he is and spare no pains to improve himself in body, mind and soul.

Gandhi[13]

[13]   Mahatma Gandhi, *The Way to God*, (Berkeley, CA: Berkeley Hills Books,1999), 43.

Chapter 8

The Gift of Self-Knowledge

T he great metaphors from all spiritual traditions such as awakening from illusion, grace, being born anew, and achieving liberation, all agree that it is possible to transcend the conditionings of our past and live our lives in a whole new way. I decided that if others had done it, I could do it too.

My goal was to heal the passive violence I had been directing toward myself. My first step was admitting that I needed to be more knowledgeable about the workings of my own mind. This is not an easy thing for most of us to admit, because as adults we take great pride in believing that we already know ourselves and there is nothing more to learn. In fact, we can become quite resistant if anyone suggests otherwise. However, our resistance is often a clue that our ego is attempting to block valuable information that can shed light on the issues we are working to heal. Our willingness to access and analyze this information is an important part of our work as evolving peacemakers.

Self-knowledge deals with the process of awakening to deeper levels of our own consciousness, transforming our character weaknesses, and discovering more of our spiritual strengths and creative potential. It is not something we master in a day, a week, or even a year. However, the more we strive for deeper self-awareness, the better able we are to uncover deeply buried emotional issues that have clouded our self-perception and caused us to act out in defensive or angry ways.

In addition, self-knowledge brings with it the awareness that we are much greater than our mistakes or accomplishments. We come to see that we have within us all the attributes we need to express our highest selves.

As we gradually liberate ourselves from our ego-centered insecurities and self-doubts, we become free to embrace a whole new way of understanding ourselves and our world. It's as though we have been living in the basement of a large house and not realizing there was an entire upper floor available to us. Self-knowledge opens the basement door and frees us to approach life in a more expanded and fulfilling way.

I began to identify some of my negative thought patterns and started working on healing the habit of using passive violence against myself. My first step was learning to accept criticism without feeling inadequate and defensive.

A Memory Brought to Life

One day as I was meditating on how to effectively handle critical feedback, a childhood memory came to mind. I hadn't thought of this incident in years, but at this time it came as a gift to remind me of a very important lesson I once learned about the fine art of constructive criticism.

When I was four years old, I was cast in a play and began my professional acting career in the theater.

The plot of the play centered around a family man and his relationships with his wife and children. I played the youngest child. Everyone in the play was experienced and understood how the rehearsal process worked. Since this was my first play, I wasn't quite sure what to expect. I was told that I would be working with a director named Bill, and his job would be to rehearse the actors, give us suggestions on how to improve our performances, and find creative ways to help the actors work effectively together. I nodded and smiled, but I don't think I understood a word they said. I just knew that Bill seemed like a very nice man and I was excited to be in the play.

Leona's professional stage debut circa 1950

On the first day of rehearsal I was called to the theater to block one of my scenes. I knew my lines and was sure I could do what was expected of me just the way I had done at the audition several weeks before.

The rehearsal began, and we started running the scene. After a few minutes, Bill told me to change the way I interpreted one of my lines. A little while later, he asked me to stop playing with my dress. Finally, he directed me to go back to the way I had read my line the first time. At this point I felt so inadequate that I started to cry. I didn't think I could do anything right.

Bill saw my distress and told the cast to take a ten-minute break. When everyone except my mom had left the room, he sat down beside me and asked why I was crying. After several attempts to speak up without sobbing, I finally told Bill that I was afraid he wouldn't let me be in the play anymore because I was doing everything wrong.

He looked at me with great compassion and in his charming English accent said, "Oh dear girl, please don't be afraid. You're not doing anything wrong."

"But you keep telling me to do different things," I cried, "so I think you don't like me and you want to get someone else to do my part."

He replied, "Of course I like you and don't want anyone else to do your part. I think you're very talented. That is exactly why I am giving you constructive criticism. Do you understand what I mean?"

"Not really," I said, feeling somewhat confused and relieved at the same time.

Bill took my hand. "Let me explain. When I hire talented actors, I see more potential in them than what they show me at their audition. I see how much better they will become with more training and coaching. I see their greatness and want to work with them to help them express themselves to the best of their ability. When I ask actors to give the scene more energy, it's because I know they can. When I see something they can do better, I try to help them by suggesting they try a different approach."

I asked, "But then, why did you want to change the way I read my first line and then change it back to the way I did it the first time? Wasn't it because I couldn't do what you wanted me to do?"

"No, not at all," he replied. "I just wanted to see how it might work a different way. After giving it some thought, I decided that the first way was more effective. Now, keep in mind I might change it again if I have a new idea for the overall tone of the scene, but remember you must not take it personally."

"Why not?" I asked. "Aren't you talking to me?"

He laughed. "Yes, but what I mean is please don't feel bad about yourself when I give you a correction. It's not because you're not good enough; it's because you're better than you think you are, and I want to help you use more of your talent. It's called constructive criticism."

I finally got it and was so grateful to Bill for taking the time to help me feel better. Soon I began to notice that he gave constructive criticism to all the actors, and every one of them improved his or her performance as the rehearsals continued. It no longer hurt my feelings when he gave me feedback. I just made the corrections and moved on. It made me feel good to know that Bill believed in me enough to give me constructive criticism that would help me grow into a better actor.

Unfortunately, not all of the feedback we receive in our formative years is constructive. As the years passed, my memory of the wonderful experience I had with Bill during my very first play receded into the background, as too many other negative experiences seemed to overshadow it.

As I grew up I saw that children can often be criticized in nonconstructive and sometimes abusive ways. Instead of teaching us to be stronger and self-confident, this type of criticism or passive violence can weaken and rob us of our sense of self-worth. Unless we take conscious steps to address our issues, we will take our emotional wounds into adulthood and unconsciously inflict them onto others.

It is not always the act of criticism that is the problem but the style of criticism and the way it is presented that can determine whether or not it is defined as passive violence. It is also our degree of emotional insecurity that determines whether or not we react negatively to what has been said to us.

One of the most challenging aspects of healing passive violence toward ourselves is learning to discern the difference between constructive and nonconstructive criticism. When we are weakened and wounded by years of bullying and hurtful language, we become overly sensitive to any type of input from others. Even a slight critique sounds like an attack to us, and we feel compelled to defend ourselves by repeatedly justifying our behavior in a desperate attempt to be right. Then we ride the emotional pendulum between condemning ourselves for giving others so much power and condemning those who criticized us. We add fuel to the flame of passive violence and feel even more like victims. As a result, we stand in the way of our own self-improvement, because we refuse to take input from others. I was determined to change that for myself.

Self-Observation and Mindfulness

As I began to learn about the many facets of self-knowledge, I saw a specific discipline that struck me as the very one I needed to start shifting my mind-set toward more constructive ways of thinking. It is called *self-observation.*

Self-observation is our inherent ability to acknowledge objectively what we are thinking, feeling, or doing at any given time. This practice has also been referred to as mindfulness or observable awareness. The understanding that part of us can remain objective, nonresistant, and nonjudgmental even in the most trying of times is dynamic and liberating. As we practice observing our thoughts, we can determine whether or not our vulnerable emotions might be interfering with the way we interpret input from others. We can also observe how often we confuse who we are with what we do and end up allowing our mistakes to define us. In other words, what we do is subject to evaluation and improvement. Who we are is always enough.

For example, we can admit that we failed at a task without calling ourselves failures. We can acknowledge that we have done things we regret without calling ourselves worthless. As we practice observing how we judge ourselves and become more mindful of the difference between critiquing our actions and demeaning our individuality, we can make significant strides in minimizing the buildup of passive violence within us. We can then begin the process of learning to communicate with ourselves in a way that helps us learn from our mistakes without berating the essence of who we are.

I started observing others to determine what healthy self-talk sounded like. I resolved to become more mindful of my own actions and evaluate them as objectively as possible without indulging in the destructive habit of shame and blame. My goal was to start using my words in healthier, more constructive ways.

I found that one of the easiest ways to learn about constructive self-evaluation is by listening to professional athletes being interviewed after a sporting event. Most of the time they give an accurate assessment of their performances without getting caught up in emotional baggage.

Instead of reproaching themselves by saying, "I was really stupid on that last play," they will say, "I did not complete that play." Instead of directing blame toward others and complaining, "It was their fault I missed the ball," they will simply report, "I did not make that catch."

The more objective they are in their self-evaluations, the better able they are to make the necessary corrections and improve their game.

Certainly the athletes might wish they had done a better job, but they cannot afford to get stuck in negative self-talk. Their priorities are to develop their skills and be effective team players, which requires focusing on the game, learning from their mistakes, and moving on. Instead of scolding themselves by saying, "I'm just no good" or "I hate myself for messing up," they make a more accurate and rational evaluation by commenting, "I will review that play and make the necessary improvements before the next game."

Looking at the same issue from a different perspective, it is important to avoid getting carried away with excessive self-praise as well. When athletes are lauded for their achievements, they will usually accept their compliments graciously without inflating them or bragging about them. Instead of putting themselves on a pedestal by claiming, "What an amazing talent I have. I'm so awesome that nobody can touch me!" they are likely to give a more balanced response, such as, "Thank you. I am grateful I was able to accomplish my goal."

Receiving praise for our work can be a most gratifying experience, as long as we don't walk away thinking we are better than others. Remember, the pendulum swings both ways between self-aggrandizement and self-condemnation. Our aim is to find a healthy balance by learning to evaluate both our successes and failures in benevolent and constructive ways without resorting to blame, shame, or the need to elevate ourselves above others. In this way we can actively heal the warring factions within ourselves and move forward in the direction of inner harmony.

After much meditation, counseling, prayer, and patience, I am becoming more objective in my self-assessments. I am forming the habit of evaluating and correcting my errors without using pejorative terminology against myself. I am also becoming more mindful of the way I respond to others who ask for my opinions of their work. As I offer loving, constructive criticism, they are more likely to feel professionally supported instead of personally diminished. It becomes a win-win situation for all concerned.

As an evolving peacemaker,

I walk the path of

inner healing.

I have learnt through bitter experience the one supreme lesson, to conserve my anger, and as heat conserved is transmuted into energy, even so, our anger controlled can be transmuted into a power which can move the world.[14]

Gandhi

[14] Gandhi, *Special session of the Congress 4–9 September 1920, Calcutta* http://sfr-21.org/sources/non-cooperation.html)

Chapter 9

Shedding Light on Anger

A nger is probably the most mysterious and misunderstood of all our emotions, because it seems so dangerous and beyond our control. Generally speaking, we don't know how to express our anger without losing our tempers and saying things we don't mean. Afterward we end up feeling guilty, confused, and angrier for having tried to speak up in the first place.

We then make efforts to push our anger out of the way, because we don't want to have more emotionally charged interactions that could potentially threaten our relationships. Sometimes we're so effective in pushing our anger down that we think it's actually gone away. Then one day a seemingly harmless comment made by a friend or family member inadvertently triggers our carefully hidden arsenal of unresolved emotions and we find ourselves exploding like a volcano. This only reinforces our belief that anger is dangerous and must be avoided at all cost.

No doubt some of our earliest and strongest memories include warnings from our parents and teachers that anger is bad and expressing it leads to serious trouble. Perhaps we even remember being physically punished because our anger got the best of us.

"Spare the rod and spoil the child" was a popular saying when I was growing up, meaning that unless children were physically reprimanded with a spanking or beating they would not learn to control their behavior. It was believed that a good spanking with a belt or switch would knock some sense into children and rid them of their rebellious ways. This theory was so widely acknowledged that even in classic Hollywood films parents are often shown spanking their children, while reciting dialogue such as, "This hurts me more than it hurts you."

I don't doubt that the adults who agreed with this philosophy were sincere in their efforts to cure their children of aggressive behavior, but I am convinced they did not foresee the devastating consequences of their actions.

The fact is that violence breeds violence. Unless we learn more about the nature of anger and develop methods of using it wisely, we will continue to suffer from the belief that whoever is the strongest and hits the hardest wins. This mind-set is both dangerous and self-defeating. As Gandhi has stated, "An eye for an eye ends in making everybody blind."[15]

Psychologists today tell us that anger is a normal emotion with a wide range of expressions. It is an energy within each of us that ranges from mild irritation to intense rage, and it can be used in a variety of ways. Anger can be used in positive ways to motivate us and move us forward in times of challenge. It is not anger that we need to eradicate, it is the erroneous belief that anger is always destructive.

Everyone experiences anger, and it can be healthy. It can motivate us to stand up for ourselves and correct injustices. When we manage anger well it prompts us to make positive changes in our lives.

Mismanaged anger, however, is counterproductive and can be unhealthy. When anger is too intense, out of control, and overly aggressive, it can lead to poor decision making, relationship challenges, difficulties in the workplace, and even health issues.

Psychologists and medical doctors have experimented with various ways of dealing with anger. Do we let it all hang out and tell it like it is, in hopes of releasing stress and feeling vindicated? Do we

---

[15] Louis Fischer, *The Life of Mahatma Gandhi*, (New York: Harper & Row,1950) 77.

regularly suppress our frustrations and avoid confrontation at all cost? Actually, neither extreme has proven to be effective.

Current research concludes that when we recognize anger as a normal emotion, observe it carefully during our daily interactions, and learn to make choices that enable us to improve our current circumstances, we can engage in effective anger management.

Remember that it is not bad or wrong to feel angry; it is how we manage it that makes the difference. Anger does not have to lead to aggression. We can learn to express our anger in respectful ways and also release its negative effects on our consciousness without having to deny or suppress our emotions.

As evolving peacemakers, it is essential that we take an objective look at the nature of anger and find ways to harness its power in healthy ways.

Lightning or Lamp?

One of the most charming and inspiring books on the subject of dealing effectively with anger is called *Grandfather Gandhi*. It is written by Arun Gandhi and Bethany Hegedus and illustrated by Evan Turk (Simon and Schuster, New York, 2014). Although the beautiful picture book is written primarily for children, it contains timeless wisdom for all generations.

The story tells of a young Arun Gandhi who visits his grandfather and learns a powerful truth about anger. After Arun almost loses control of his anger during a game with other children, Grandfather Gandhi tells him that anger is like lightning. It has the power to split a tree in half or it can become luminous and turn the darkness into light. Each of us can choose to flip the switch inside of us and turn the lightning into a lamp. We are responsible for making that choice each day, by consciously working to use our anger in positive ways instead of allowing it to get the best of us. Arun tells us at the end of the book that he makes this choice every day of his life.

Flipping the Switch

As I look back on key moments of my life, I remember a number of occasions when, without knowing what to call it, I chose to flip the switch inside of me and turn the lightning into a lamp.

One of my most memorable opportunities occurred when I was a young teenager studying dance. I wanted so much to glide gracefully across the stage and perform skillfully before large and appreciative audiences. I daydreamed about it constantly and looked forward to my weekly class.

After I had been studying for about six months, I learned that the studio was hosting a special recital in which every student would have a chance to solo in front of the other classes. I eagerly looked forward to my first recital and was excited for my chance to show everyone what a good dancer I was.

On the day of the show I practically counted the minutes until all the students took their places and it was time to begin. The advanced class performed their solos first and then the intermediates. Finally, it was my turn. I carefully took my position at the center of the stage and waited for my music to begin. Soon I was out there performing my dance and enjoying every bit of it.

A few moments into my routine, however, I felt the ribbons on one of my ballet slippers coming loose. Before I knew it I had tripped over them and fallen flat on my face.

For a few moments there was dead silence, while I slowly picked myself up and made sure I wasn't hurt. Then the laughter started. At first there was a single giggle, then a few more, and soon waves of hysterical laughter were reverberating throughout the studio. I stood there mortified until our instructor eventually managed to silence the outburst. She helped me tie my slipper and gently encouraged me to start my dance again from the top. I reluctantly agreed to give it another shot.

As I attempted to steady my nerves and get into position, one of the students shouted out, "What difference does it make? She's no good anyway."

Several of the students started laughing again. By now I was so mortified that I ran out of the studio and swore I would never dance again.

Over the next few months I felt rage toward that student. Not only had she started the laughter when I fell down but she had humiliated me in front of everyone by making that cruel comment. I wanted to punch her out. I wanted to see her down on the floor as I had been. I wanted to be the one laughing at her. I imagined all kinds of situations where I would exact my revenge and make her beg for my forgiveness. It was a very dark period for me.

After a while I realized how much I missed my dance classes, and I blamed her for that too. She was the one who was taking my dreams away. She was the one who was keeping me from being happy. She was the one who—wait a minute. That wasn't true. The reality was that I could go back to class anytime I wanted. She didn't have the power to take away my dream; I was the one who was doing that. In fact, every time I relived the events of the recital in my mind, I was actually giving her permission to ridicule me all over again.

Eventually I began to release my obsessive need to get even. Slowly the echoes of laughter and humiliation faded away, and something else took over. I made up my mind that I wanted to dance and that I *would* dance. I would practice diligently and improve my technique. I would shift my energy from being an angry victim to perfecting my work and following my dream in a way that I had never done before.

Soon I went back to dance class with a fierce determination to work hard and keep focused on what I wanted to accomplish. I had more energy than ever and instead of dancing once a week I took a class every day. I sought out mentors to help me hone my skills and practiced every chance I could get.

About two years later I was chosen to dance at a special event and found myself working with the student who had laughed at me. I had been avoiding her all this time, but now I was glad to see her. In fact, I was grateful to her. I realized that had she not ridiculed me that day I might not have realized how much work it would take for me to become a dancer. I was now able to see her as a teacher not an enemy. Out of the corner of my eye I saw her approach me tentatively. I turned and smiled at her. We gave each other a hug, made our peace, and began our rehearsal.

Eventually I began a long and rewarding career in professional musical theater and got the opportunity to live my dream!

Leona (center) as the oldest daughter, Tzeitel,
Fiddler on the Roof (Caesar's Palace, Las Vegas, 1968)

It took me years to realize that the energy I had invested in resentment toward my classmate was the same energy that gave me the drive and self-discipline to work hard and develop my talents.

The more we understand the nature of anger the less we fear it. Instead, we learn to respect it and seek out ways to transform its destructive tendencies into constructive, positive action. It is our choice as well as our responsibility to turn the lightning into a lamp and use our anger in constructive ways.

Of course this shift in consciousness takes a great deal of dedication and fortitude. Fortunately, we are up to the task.

As an evolving peacemaker,

I walk the path of

self-discipline.

Chapter 10

Turning Lightning into a Lamp

by Matthew J. Evans

I have always admired my mom and her work in the theater. Whenever I'd hear her stories of traveling across the country and performing for people, I'd get really excited and imagine myself doing the same thing. What I didn't fully realize was that the entertainment business is full of highs and lows. For every job my mom got, there were many she didn't. That's true for every person in show business. Whether you're an actor, musician, dancer, or director, you are always losing way more jobs than you're booking. My mom knew this firsthand, of course, because she lived that life for thirty years. She experienced the joys of success and feeling accomplished in her art, but she also knew what it felt like to feel completely defeated and frustrated when the role she wanted so desperately went to someone else.

When I decided at the age of nine that I wanted to be a professional actor on film and television, my mom had some trepidation. She didn't want me to completely hinge my self-worth on whether I booked a role or had the highest billing, and she especially didn't want me to become angry, resentful, and depressed from the hundreds of inevitable *no's* I would receive. I assured her it wouldn't happen to me.

We signed with an agency in Los Angeles, and I started going out on auditions. It was really fun. I got great feedback and started booking roles on several television programs and a feature film. I loved the work, everything was great, and I thought I'd be a star in no time.

As I got older, though, I booked jobs less often. I still auditioned a lot, but the jobs were coming much less frequently. I was growing taller than most kids my age, and when you're a child actor, the younger you look the better. There were several auditions that I can remember at which I got down to the final two or three kids, but since I was almost as tall as the actors who were playing my dad, I didn't get the parts. Even without the height problem, I was just booking less in general. It was really starting to get to me, and I began to get caught up in feelings of anger and rejection.

One experience in particular stands out as being especially difficult and memorable for me. I was trying out for a lead role in a feature film that I really wanted. I was the right age and had the right look. I worked really hard on the audition piece, got some professional coaching, and was doing very well with the material. It was a comedy, and I definitely felt the timing and the delivery. The whole character was coming together perfectly.

I got to the audition, and the casting directors loved my performance. They were laughing like crazy and they said I was fantastic. I got a callback and met with the director.

The two of us hit it off instantly. The director said I was absolutely perfect for the part and he wanted to work with me. He coached me for the audition tape he was taking to the producers and said he loved my work. Of course I assumed this meant I had the part in the bag, and I was thrilled.

A little while later I got a call saying they wanted to do more auditions. The director was being superseded by the producing team, who felt that he had decided too quickly without their input. My agent said I would be invited to the final callback the following week. I was so committed to getting this part that I actually dyed my hair to totally get into character. The callback day arrived, and I went down for what I assumed was a formality to lock in my part.

When I got to the studio, there were two other guys trying out for what I believed was *my* part. When it was my turn, I walked into the audition room, sure I would do my best and wow the producers.

If you haven't heard of a "dead room" before, it's a show business term for when the audience doesn't give any kind of response. It's one of the scariest things a performer can go through, and this audition room was deader than anything I'd ever experienced in my entire acting career. The producers seemed to stare at me blankly, and they didn't say a word. I was really uncomfortable but still thought I did a good job.

After the audition was over, I got out of the room as fast as I could. I was furious. I felt betrayed by the director for leading me to believe I had the part when it wasn't his decision alone to make. I was angry at the producers for not seeing that I was right person for the part. I was really angry with myself because it felt as if I had put so much work and passion into my audition and it still wasn't good enough. It made me feel that *I* wasn't good enough, and the whole situation really got me down.

My mom saw what I was going through. She recognized the same feelings of pain, disappointment, and anger that she had gone through herself. I know it must have been hard for her. She was seeing me go through the exact thing she'd wanted me to avoid.

Luckily she was there for me and helped me work through my issues. She gave me some incredible advice, which is something I have to remind myself of every day.

She told me there are certain things in my work that I can control and certain things I can't. For example, I can study the character. I can make sure I learn my lines. I can take the time to understand the script and know the story. I can be responsible for having recent professional photographs and an up-to-date resume. I can be dressed appropriately for the character.

I can also control whether or not I practice my acting skills and my life skills. Do I take professional acting classes? Do I feel confident and secure in my ability to do a great job with the role if I book it? Do I have a positive attitude? Am I willing to learn a valuable lesson from an experience, no matter what the outcome? She told me that when I have answered yes to all of those questions, then I can rest assured I have done everything I can to perform a successful audition. Those are the things I can control.

However, I also need to know there are things I can't control. I can't control whether or not I get the job. I can't force the director or producer to hire me. I can't control whether they like my performance or if I fit their vision for the character. All I can do is my best at any particular time and afterward let it go.

My mom also gave me an affirmation to say after every audition: "This or something better." This means that I become less attached to the outcome of a particular situation and remember that I have a bright future ahead of me even if I can't exactly predict how it's going to take place.

If I understand these things, I can stop taking every rejection so personally and use my feelings of anger and frustration to keep me moving toward my goal.

Also my mom said that I needed to learn at least one thing from every audition I attended. If it was a great audition, what made it so amazing? If it was a bad audition, what did or didn't I do to keep me from doing my best? She said it was very important to stick to the facts and not get into shame or blame when I was evaluating my audition. This is a really valuable tool, because it requires honest self-reflection and a lot of discipline.

I've been working on these ideas a lot in the past few years. They apply to all areas of life, not just acting. I've learned that turning anger into something positive takes a lot of practice but is definitely worth the effort, because when I am willing to apply the principles, it's really powerful.

The hardest change I needed to make was getting over the feeling that if I didn't book a role it meant that I was a failure. My mom kept reminding me that having failed at something didn't mean that *I* was a failure. It just meant that I had something else to learn from that experience. She also reminded me of how many roles I had actually booked and that if I really wanted to do this work I had to make peace with the whole unpredictable process. I needed to remember to use my anger in positive ways so that I would have the strength to further my goals.

Once I could see past the problem, I was able to really dig into what I could learn from these situations. The self-observation became easier when I wasn't beating myself up. I could say, "You know, my delivery of the lines was good, but I just didn't physically carry myself like the character should" or "I wasn't prepared enough on my lines and I stumbled a few times. I'll work on those skills for next time." When I'm able to just observe myself and take a reality check, I can really learn a lot.

I had to work a lot with my mom on these issues. After that one really disappointing audition when I was sure I had booked the job, I gave some serious thought to giving up acting altogether. It was a very sad time. I really didn't want to give it up, but I didn't want to feel heartbroken and angry anymore either. I knew if I quit my acting career I would regret it. I'd walk away frustrated that I'd been beaten by the business. I'd regret giving up on an art form that I cared so much about.

Eventually I was able to come back to what my mom had said: "There are certain things in life we can control and certain things we can't control." Then I started thinking back on the final day of that audition. I had certainly been prepared enough. I had known all the lines backwards and forwards, and I had looked the part—but what had happened?

As I mentioned earlier in the chapter, it looked as if the producers had been staring daggers at me. I don't know if this was really true, but it had felt that way, and I had let my feelings affect my performance in a negative way. It was hard to admit at first, but once I did, I could begin the process of figuring out what I could do to change my attitude.

I finally decided that from then on I needed to practice being fully focused on my task and not be distracted by others or allow them to intimidate me. No matter who is in the audience or how much their approval means to me, my number-one priority must be to express my talents to the best of my ability and let my light shine. This has been a very important lesson for me, and I am grateful that I could find something valuable in that difficult experience.

Another important thing happened following that event. I remembered that I had other talents that I could devote my attention to, such as filmmaking and music. I continued to audition and act in film and television, but I began focusing more attention on my other passion, music. I had already been studying electric bass, but I also began learning upright bass. Today I devote a lot of time to studying and performing jazz music, and it brings me so much joy. It's just as important to me as my acting, and it's provided a constant creative outlet that balances really well with my acting work.

In a situation where I had let my anger get the best of me, I was able (with help) to use the anger in a positive way. If I had allowed myself to be overwhelmed and quit acting, I would've been filled with regret at giving up what I loved. I also would have ended up blaming myself and every director who ever passed me up. No matter what else happened in my life, somewhere in the back of my mind would be the anger that was left unhealed. I didn't want to live the rest of my life that way. Now I understand that I don't have to. I can make different choices.

Within me is the potential to change my perspective, pull myself out of anger and despair, and forge ahead stronger with a new outlook. It's within everyone.

I've been to a number of auditions since that time. I've booked some roles and have been passed up for others. The main thing is that I'm practicing being an evolving peacemaker by remembering to control what I can, not stressing about what I can't, and finding valuable lessons in the experience. As Grandfather Gandhi said, I can make the choice to turn lightning into a lamp.

Mathew, age 10

Young Artist Award, Supporting
Young Actor in a Feature
Film, Bad Teacher (2012)

Matthew J. Evans, bassist (2016)

Young Artist Award, Guest-
Starring Young Actor in a
TV Series, Lab Rats (2014)

As an evolving peacemaker,

I walk the path of

healthy self-expression.

Chapter 11

The Consequences of Concealed Anger

When something angers us, it is important to be honest with ourselves and acknowledge our feelings. We don't need to express our anger nor should we attempt to ignore it. We just need to recognize it for what it is. As we have stated in previous chapters, anger is energy and, as evolving peacemakers, we have a responsibility to identify this energy and direct it in useful and nonviolent ways.

Anger can also be a sign that something inside of us is wounded and needs to be healed. This is one reason why we don't want to misuse this powerful energy by suppressing it or turning it against ourselves. Our goal is to heal our anger, not give it a permanent home in our consciousness.

Too often we have a hard time admitting that we carry anger inside of us, because we are afraid of it and have not had much success with our attempts to express it. However, the more we deny our pent-up frustrations the easier it becomes to slip into passive-aggressive behaviors, which can frequently cause more harm than good.

Passive-aggressive behavior is a form of passive violence that occurs when we are unwilling or unable to take responsibility for our anger and without realizing it find subtle and indirect ways to make ourselves heard.

"I will do anything to avoid confrontation" is a commonly used statement. But this can lead to negative and unexpected consequences if we habitually stuff our angry feelings and allow them to build up inside of us.

Much of our anger buildup stems from a fear of confrontation and the challenges that could result from such action. Often, burying our anger is linked with issues of perfectionism, which include unrealistic expectations of ourselves and others.

If we don't find constructive ways to deal with our anger, we will eventually go into denial, which results in a separation between our feelings and our behavior. Whenever there is a disconnect between what we say (passive) and what we do (aggressive) we inadvertently build up more anger and frustration, which generates more passive-aggressive behavior and takes us further away from the peace we so deeply desire.

Passive-aggressive behavior is an indirect and often unconscious form of communication that occurs when we attempt to express our unresolved anger without verbalizing it directly. Instead we use subtle and indirect behaviors to demonstrate our displeasure.

Unfortunately, rather than making our needs known, we inadvertently create frustration and misunderstanding for all parties involved. This is why it is especially important to observe our words and behaviors and ask ourselves periodically whether or not we have any anger issues that need to be healed.

Passive-aggressive behaviors are recognizable and fairly simple to identify once we know what we are looking for. This is why it is important to take a look at some of the classic behaviors and learn all we can about finding and healing any residual anger from our past.

Please keep in mind that passive-aggressive behavior is a very common way to deal with unresolved anger and is not confined to any particular segment of humanity. This behavior is common to all of us, and the sooner we address it in ourselves the better able we will be to "turn the lightning into a lamp" and use our pent-up energy in positive ways.

We can manifest passive-aggressive behavior in the following ways:

- habitual forgetfulness

- procrastination

- chronic lateness

- stubbornness

- backhanded compliments

- sarcasm

- inappropriate humor

- agreeing to perform a task and not following through

- praising people to their faces and then criticizing them behind their backs

- getting upset with someone and not saying why

These are some of the behaviors that can point to a passive-aggressive approach to problem solving. The real issues are never addressed, and our underlying anger is not acknowledged. Both parties have a strong sense that something is wrong but can't seem to identify the problem correctly, which then exacerbates the unspoken tension in the relationship. Learning to identify and take responsibility for our own feelings gives us the freedom to make more informed choices, as we learn to deal effectively with our anger.

Choosing the Right Approach

In situations where our problem is aggression (active violence), we can use appropriate anger management tools such as these:

- choosing to leave the room when feeling overwhelmed so that we don't lash out at others

- making an agreement to discuss the situation at a later time when we are feeling less volatile

- keeping a journal to become more aware of events that trigger a negative response in us

- joining a support group that is accepting and works constructively with our challenges

- using meditation and relaxation techniques on a regular basis

- seeing a therapist who specializes in anger management

These methods can support us in dealing with the causes of our anger and move us in the direction of mastering our emotions.

In cases of passive-aggressive behavior (passive violence) traditional anger management tools aren't as effective, because we don't acknowledge our anger. We continue to believe it is others who have the problem and if they would only change their ways we would be fine.

How Do We Treat a Problem We Don't Know We Have?

Recently I was able to admit that an issue I struggled with for many years was really passive-aggressive in nature. The problem manifested as chronic tardiness, but the cause was rooted in an underlying anger and frustration that I was not able to identify.

Working on this section of the book provided me with the necessary insights to make an important connection between the symptom (lateness) and the cause (anger). Prior to this discovery, I was not open to taking full responsibility for my ongoing tardiness, because from my perspective, I always had a good excuse for being late. It was never really my fault.

My time issues became noticeable when I got into high school. We didn't have school buses, so I either had to walk to school, which was about a mile and a half from our house, or take a city bus.

Every morning when my alarm rang I resisted getting out of bed. When I finally did get up, I had to rush like crazy to get to school. On the few occasions when I arrived on time, it felt as though I had beaten the odds and scored a victory, but most times I was late.

It's not that I wanted to be tardy. I really just wanted to sleep later. In fact, I really didn't like walking into a class after it began. I would sort of tiptoe into the room with my eyes downcast and sense the disapproval of those around me. Then I would feel ashamed of my behavior and apologize profusely, making all kinds of excuses for why it had happened.

Sometimes I seemed to get away with being late. Other times I would receive a lecture from a frustrated teacher complaining that my tardiness was a sign of careless, rude, and disrespectful behavior.

The teacher would then go on to extoll the virtues of promptness and give me examples of great heroes throughout history who always met their obligations in a timely way. These lectures would always end with an admonition for me to behave in a more responsible way and live up to my considerable potential.

I must admit here that while I was genuinely ashamed of my behavior, a part of me used to get a kick out of the "great heroes" part. It seemed like overkill. Nevertheless, I was quick to assure all those involved that it would never happen again and that I was determined to change my ways. My apologies were always sincere, and I convinced myself that I could and would keep my promises.

After each of those embarrassing lectures, I made an extra effort to arrive at school before the first class began. On my best days I usually managed to get there a minute or two before the bell rang, huffing and puffing from having run the last few blocks. After a few weeks, however, I would gradually start sliding back into my old familiar ways.

I didn't realize how often I was late during high school until I received an end-of-semester report card one year and noticed that out of one hundred school days I was marked tardy sixty-seven times. That was a bit of a shock, but since the information didn't go on my transcript, I didn't think it was a big deal. After all, I studied long hours and worked really hard, often late into the night, for everything I accomplished. Didn't I deserve a break? Who cared if I was a few minutes late? (Notice how I vacillated between remorse and self-justification.)

Eventually both the teachers and students stopped paying attention to whether I was late or not. Perhaps my consistently high grades and other notable activities outside of school put my time issues on a back burner. One day, however, an article about my theatrical achievements came out in the school newspaper and changed all that. The writer, a classmate of mine and editor of the paper, closed the piece by saying: "Leona, you are very talented, and I know you'll have great success in life. I just hope you're on time for it."

Everyone at school got a big kick out of that line. I enjoyed it too, not only because it was funny but now I could actually continue to show up late to school and amuse my friends at the same time. From then on, whenever I showed up late my classmates would sneak little smiles at me, and I didn't feel ashamed anymore.

A Look Back in Time

Where did my time issues come from? Everyone in my family was highly disciplined when it came to promptness. They felt it was a virtue to arrive not only on time but *early* to every appointment, whether it was business or social. When I was a small child, my objection to being early was that once we got to our destination, after an average two-hour ride on a Chicago city bus, we often had to wait around before anything got started. During these excursions I often felt cranky and irritable. I was exhausted from the traveling and wanted to be carried instead of having to walk.

Soon I grew too big to be carried (portable lightweight strollers were not yet available). Needless to say, I was quite disagreeable anytime I had to travel by bus and would constantly complain, "Why do we have to wait so long for the bus?" "Why can't we take a taxi?" "Why can't you buy a car?"

After hearing enough whining and complaining, my parents would severely reprimand me for being ungrateful and displaying a bad temper. How vividly I remember those times.

If I had been several years older and easier to reason with, I might have been open to listening to my parents' point of view. I might have accepted the idea that we can't always have our own way and there are times when we have to make the best of unpleasant situations whether we like them or not. However, this is a fairly sophisticated concept that even adults have a problem accepting.

The fact is that I was a very small child who did not have the maturity to take a rational approach to the travel problem. I was too young to see that my parents did not have the money to buy a car or take a taxi to our destinations.

Eventually I stopped complaining, and my family thought I had made peace with the situation. Apparently I had just buried my anger so deeply it seemed to disappear.

Of course I am very grateful to my parents for getting me to my acting jobs in a timely way when I was a child. Their responsible and professional behavior assured that I would be wherever I was supposed to be. My parents and grandparents were honest, hardworking people who expected the best from themselves and instilled in me a high work ethic, which included preparation, promptness, and respect for my profession. Out of all the valuable life lessons they provided for me, however, the one I strongly rebelled against was the importance of promptness.

As I grew to young adulthood and began going places on my own, I developed a strategy that I believed would get me to any destination at the exact moment I was due. No longer would I have to arrive so early for every meeting and wait around for what seemed like an eternity.

This was my plan. If my scheduled appointment was at 10:00 a.m., I would plan to arrive at *exactly* 10:00 a.m. I carefully structured my travel time to the minute. For example, if my meeting was ten miles away and the average driving time was one mile a minute, I figured a taxi could get me there in ten minutes.

Strangely enough, I didn't see the flaws in this plan even though most of the time it didn't work and I ended up being late. In those instances, I was sure the driver had been moving too slowly or there had been unexpected traffic, rain, roadwork, or flat tires that prevented me from arriving on time.

When I explained my strategy for being on time to my friends and co-workers, they were amazed at my naivety. Some of them expressed bewilderment as they questioned how someone as smart as I was could come up with such a flawed plan.

At first I reacted defensively to their input, but eventually I realized it was all part of the classic passive-aggressive mentally. I could come up with all sorts of ways to arrive on time, and even make sincere efforts to show up on time, but if unconsciously I resented having to *be* on time, my efforts became little more than self-defeating behaviors. It was so confusing, and I never seemed to get to the root of the problem.

After a while my chronic lateness started having a negative impact on my professional life, and I began a series of counseling sessions to determine the cause of my problem. After a few visits, my counselor told me that I had "a poor relationship with time." He explained that in addition to my ineffective strategy of trying to arrive places at the precise moment they were scheduled, I also tended to cram too many activities into my day. Unfortunately, I seldom accomplished them all and was constantly frustrated and overwhelmed.

The counselor's assessment made perfect sense to me. I was always putting too many things on my to-do list, causing me to rush around trying to get things done. I seldom managed to accomplish everything and often found myself exhausted and frustrated at the end of the day. I could now see that there were legitimate reasons why I was so often late; I decided to fix my problem by simply eliminating some of my daily routines. This would leave more time to get to my most important appointments.

Oh, how I wish it had been that simple. It turned out that creating a new schedule and giving myself more time to get to my appointments only addressed the symptoms, not the problem itself. It was like advising someone with a chronic overeating problem, "Just don't put fattening foods in your refrigerator, and you will lose weight." It makes sense at some level and it might even be effective in the short term, but unless the underlying causes for the behavior are addressed, we are unlikely to see any lasting changes.

Even so, I thought I could fix my habitual lateness by cutting some unnecessary activities out of my schedule. Once again, it worked for a while, but after a couple of months I started falling back into my old behavior patterns.

It took a while before I noticed that even though I had fewer appointments I still wasn't leaving my house until the very last minute. Sometimes I just couldn't get my makeup right. Sometimes I couldn't find my keys. Sometimes I couldn't settle on the right clothes to wear. More often than not I overslept and woke up in a panic, knowing that there was no way I could arrive on time. Other times I went to bed late, woke up exhausted, and couldn't function quickly enough to get ready. Of course these things didn't happen every day, just often enough for me to gain a reputation that a few people found amusing and most found infuriating.

Those who objected to my lateness objected strongly. They would accuse me of being selfish, inconsiderate, and disrespectful for wasting their time. Although I always responded by being contrite and apologetic, a part of me simply couldn't understand why they reacted so strongly. I figured that being late was just a bad habit and had nothing to do with anyone else. I would attempt to justify my behavior by saying, "It's just a flaw in my personality; please don't take it personally. It's really not about you; I've been this way all my life." Meanwhile, I would think to myself, *It's only ten minutes— what's the big deal?*

When I became aware of the conflict within my own consciousness, I went back to counseling. I really didn't want to appear irresponsible to others and at this point was highly motivated to gain mastery over my continual battle with time.

During the sessions with my new therapist, I made more changes to my daily routine. I began laying out my clothes the night before, attaching my keys to my purse, making sure all my materials were ready for the following day, and setting two alarm clocks to assure that I would awaken on time. In addition, I found help with the new GPS technology and was now able to figure the approximate length of time to my destinations, taking traffic time into consideration.

In addition to behavior modification, my therapist helped me delve more deeply into my personal issues, especially those involving anger. The more issues we uncovered, the better able I was to admit that my chronic lateness was in many instances rooted in unresolved anger. While I wasn't exactly sure what all of my anger was about, I knew now that the situation was important enough to address seriously. I also knew that it was within my power to find and heal whatever was buried in the recesses of my consciousness.

Even though I still couldn't always identify the specific areas in which I was resistant, I became more willing to catch myself before falling into my old behavior patterns. As a result, I have grown considerably throughout the years, and most of the time I manage to arrive at my destinations in a timely way—on rare occasions even a little early. The rest of the puzzle pieces came together only recently.

Stepping Out of the Shadows

For the past few months I have been working diligently on researching passive-aggressive behavior in hopes of shedding more light on the issues of passive violence. More often than not I found myself taking time off from writing to delve more deeply into this complicated subject. Not surprisingly, I soon began to notice more and more passive-aggressive behavior in those around me. I could see how their ways of communicating with others were having negative effects on their personal and professional relationships. I could also sense how protective they were about keeping their anger under control, certain that no one else could notice it. In addition, I saw individuals who were in such deep denial that they refused to admit they had any anger whatsoever.

It was easy to see passive-aggressive behavior in those around me and it was even easier to criticize it. However, my biggest insight occurred one day when I realized that the behaviors I was criticizing in others were the same ones I needed to heal in myself!

Soon the process that began with my question "How can I help others understand and heal their passive-aggressive behavior?" shifted to "How can I understand and heal my own passive-aggressive behaviors?"

After some serious and lengthy meditations, I made an important but disturbing discovery. I finally realized that for many years I had been carrying unresolved anger toward those whom I believed were making excessive and unreasonable demands on my time. The way I rebelled against those demands was to arrive late to my appointments with them and then blame my tardiness on outside circumstances. This way it was never my fault and I never had to confront my anger, either to them or to myself. Although I was unaware of what I was doing, I was still responsible for my actions. Sadly, it all seemed to make sense.

Admitting that I had been acting out my anger toward others in a passive-aggressive manner was very painful for me. I had always prided myself on being the fully conscious person who faced and dealt with life's issues through direct communication. Obviously this was not entirely true, and the discovery was very disappointing.

I had very little patience for the passive-aggressive style in others, because I could never really be sure where I stood or what the real problem was. I was always getting mixed messages, and I could sense a distinct separation between what these individuals said they would do and what they actually did. Of course, when I would bring these discrepancies to their attention, they would seem not to understand what I was talking about or would accuse me of trying to make trouble. I strongly suspected that there were underlying anger issues that kept them from being more forthcoming and efficient, but I could never get them to admit this. When I would push for answers, hoping for a deeper level of communication, they would generally respond with resistance, often claiming that the only real problem they had was my nagging. The more I probed the harder they would resist, until I eventually had to give up or blow up.

Clearly, I resented passive-aggressive behavior. I had no respect for people who would act out in ways that hurt or frustrated others and then refuse to take responsibility for their actions. This is why it was so hard to recognize and accept the same behaviors in myself.

I didn't want to accept the idea that I was someone who would keep others waiting because I childishly believed that my time was more valuable than theirs. I didn't want to be the person who showed up late because I resented being at everyone's beck and call, working so hard and never having time for myself. I didn't want to be the person who would hold a grudge against someone who had hurt my feelings and keep them waiting as a way to get even. Finally, I desperately didn't want to be the person who still felt anger toward my wonderful parents because they didn't have enough money to buy a car when I was a child.

But I *was* that person, and my anger was begging to be brought into the light, to be embraced and transformed.

I am now going through a healing process that is both painful and necessary. This involves getting to know myself at a deeper level and awakening to more ways of becoming less judgmental and more lenient with myself and others. This is part of an ongoing journey toward greater self-acceptance and inner peace.

I am thankful that I can now feel a greater compassion for those who use passive-aggressive behavior as a way of dealing with anger. I used to judge them harshly. Now I am learning more about what motivates them—I mean *us*. The truth is, despite the many differences that exist within the human race, we are far more alike than we think.

Reflections

Anger is a power to be harnessed rather than a personality flaw to be eliminated. Once we change the way we look at anger, we can start learning to manage it instead of wasting our energy trying to extinguish it. Gradually, as we grow more honest with ourselves, we can become able to accept responsibility for our own feelings and begin communicating with others in more authentic and loving ways.

My intention in writing this book was to help others find peace within themselves and to be a positive voice for nonviolence in the world. What a special blessing it is that during this process I also am finding greater peace within myself.

As an evolving peacemaker,

I walk the path of

humility.

A man is but the product of his thoughts. What he thinks he becomes.[16]

Gandhi

---

[16]   Mahatma Gandhi *Ethical Religion*, (Madras: S. Ganesan, 1922), 62

Chapter 12

The Art of Self-Acceptance

O ur beliefs act as filters through which we determine what is true and what is not. When our filters become clogged with years of unresolved anger and self-condemnation we end up with a distorted view of ourselves and the world around us. For example, if we believe we can't trust ourselves, we will feel insecure about trusting those around us. If we believe we are superior to others, we will look down upon people as inferior. If we believe we constantly need to defend ourselves, we will see the world as a battleground. If we believe we are unworthy of being loved, we will find rejection wherever we look.

As evolving peacemakers, we want to take responsibility for changing the filter of our mind-set and lifting our consciousness to a place where we no longer struggle with issues of unworthiness, denial, or a distorted sense of reality. One of the most effective ways of achieving this goal is through self-acceptance.

Self-acceptance begins with the understanding that life, itself, is sacred and worthy of respect and compassion. The more willing we are to acknowledge that our lives have value, the easier it is to discern the difference between who we are and what we do.

Accepting ourselves does not mean we must approve of everything we do. We just need to acknowledge that we do it. Otherwise we will continue to be at war with ourselves and fail in our efforts to make real and lasting changes.

Nathaniel Branden, a twentieth century psychologist who is highly regarded for his work on the subject of self-esteem, states, "Self-acceptance is the refusal to be in an adversarial relationship with our own nature."[17]

The practice of self-acceptance allows us to experience rather than deny whatever is true about ourselves at any given time. It gives us the courage to remain present to the reality of our own behaviors, and it frees us to recognize the many and varied aspects of our personality without self-hatred or self-rejection.

Although there are those who would say that self-acceptance gives us an excuse to avoid improving ourselves, the opposite is true.

We cannot correct a problem we refuse to acknowledge. We cannot learn from a mistake we deny having made. We cannot heal anger we will not admit we possess. We cannot forgive ourselves for an action we insist we haven't taken.

We are growing and evolving every moment of our lives, and refining our character flaws is a natural part of this process. However, if we choose to justify our faults or attempt to disown them, we not only fail to learn valuable lessons but risk ending up with a lethal buildup of unbridled energy that becomes buried in our unconscious minds. This accumulation of energy is often referred to as the dark side or the shadow within us.

Meeting Our Shadow

The shadow refers to all of the qualities within us that society tells us must be eliminated or denied. During our formative years we are constantly taught which of our characteristics are acceptable and which are not. We are told that the positive ones must be cultivated into our personalities and the undesirable ones eliminated. To a certain degree these lessons are a necessary part of the socialization process and provide us with important guidelines that can teach us to interact with one another in appropriate and socially acceptable ways.

---

[17]   Nathaniel Branden, *Six Pillars of Self-Esteem* (New York, Bantam Books, 1994)

Unfortunately, there is a dangerous downside to being told we must get rid of our anger, fear, aggression, or any other quality associated with our dark side. Namely, it can't be done. We cannot dispose of our unwanted characteristics, because they are made up of energy which, according to the first law of thermodynamics (a version of the law of conservation of energy), can neither be created nor destroyed, only changed in form. This means there is nowhere for those unacceptable characteristics to go except into the unconscious part of our minds. Just because we have disowned them doesn't mean they have disappeared. Instead, they remain within us, seething beneath the surface of our consciousness. Eventually when there is too much buildup of the shadow, it bursts forth when we least expect it, causing us to lose our tempers or act out in ways that eventually bring us added shame and self-rejection.

Furthermore, attempting to rid ourselves of the shadow side of our nature is much like throwing the baby out with the bathwater. The more of the powerful aspects of our own nature we reject the stronger our shadow becomes, leaving us weakened and unable to find and access our inner strength. Just as Dr. Jekyll tried to eliminate his dark side and was eventually overtaken by Mr. Hyde, so are we diminished when we try to disown some of the more potent aspects of our own personalities. Unless we learn to acknowledge and constructively allow our shadow to embrace the light, it will manifest in unfortunate and destructive ways that can wreak havoc on our relationships with others.

Projection

One of the most lethal ways our shadow can manifest is in the form of projection. This occurs when we are so out of touch with our dark side that we become convinced that the characteristics we have pushed into our own shadow now belong exclusively to others. Projection can occur toward an individual or a group. "They" have the problem. "They" are inferior. "They" are causing all the trouble. "They" are the ones who must be eliminated.

It is dangerous to all concerned when we make others bear our shadow for us. Projection takes place in our families when a relative is labeled as the black sheep and is continually scorned by the other family members. It can also occur in neighborhoods where one family becomes a scapegoat and is ridiculed and shunned by the others. We can observe it in schools, when we see bullies violently projecting their own feelings of inadequacy and self-alienation onto those who don't seem able to defend themselves. Unfortunately, in addition to the existence of our individual shadow, there is another aspect of the shadow that we share with everyone.

The collective shadow is a compilation of energy that is part of our universal collective consciousness. Throughout history we have projected our collective rage on religions, ethnicities, political groups, and entire countries. We appease our unconscious wrath by blaming those we don't even know for all that is wrong in our world, until no one is safe and violence erupts everywhere around us.

The more vehemently we direct our anger toward others in what we believe to be righteousness indignation, the further away we are from acknowledging the anger within ourselves. Our only hope lies in taking our power back through self-acceptance and transforming our dark side into the light. As we accept ourselves in our entirety, we become able to accept others.

Coping with Resistance

After so many years of believing that parts of ourselves were unacceptable and needed to be buried, we are now being asked to recognize and accept them. Clearly this is easier said than done, especially when some of those aspects of consciousness have been buried so deeply inside of us that we don't know where to look.

One of our biggest challenges in dealing with our shadow is that we fear the power it contains. We're afraid that if we give it permission to surface, as Dr. Jekyll did, we will not be able to control it. While this is a legitimate concern, there are many ways we can reach out for support from psychologists, spiritual mentors, and friends as we grow to accept our dark side. Of course this is not something that happens all at once, but it is a necessary part of our journey toward uniting and healing the fragmented aspects of our consciousness.

Another reason for our resistance is that we feel deep shame about having to acknowledge our dark side. We really don't want to know what's in there, and we certainly don't want others to know. Nevertheless, as we progress in our journey toward self-acceptance, we come to understand that we are more than the sum of our mistakes.

A major part of our resistance is based on the mistaken belief that we have to be perfect to be lovable. The truth is that we *are* lovable, even though we have imperfections. The more fully we accept ourselves, the more effectively we can deal with those imperfections while learning to treat ourselves with compassion.

The most problematic form of resistance we can encounter on our path toward self-acceptance is our reluctance to admit that we possess the qualities we find so unacceptable in others. It is so much easier to complain about another's intolerance than to see intolerance in ourselves.

Eventually we come to see that we cannot resist the dark side without diminishing the light as well. The shadow contains much more than negativity. Within the spectrum of our consciousness lies a wealth of untapped potential that can be described as our higher calling or spiritual potential. Carl Jung, esteemed twentieth-century psychologist, referred to this latent power as "the gold in the shadow." By accepting and harnessing our dark side, we open a way for the gold to be mined and brought to the surface. We then become free to access greater levels of love and light, to sustain us as we move toward a culture of peace.

Owning Our Shadow

In the wonderful children's book called *Grandfather Gandhi*, which we discussed in a previous chapter, young Arun learns an important lesson about anger from his grandfather. Arun learns that anger is energy. It can take the form of lightning, which can split a tree, or become a lamp, which brings brilliance and light. It is up to each of us to make the choice as to how we will use that energy.

Grandfather Gandhi gave Arun one of the most important lessons we can ever learn. It is not the energy itself that is inherently bad or wrong but the way it is used. The method Gandhi used to handle the situation with Arun was a beautiful example of nonviolence and acceptance.

He did not punish Arun for letting his anger get the best of him, nor did he admonish Arun for being a bad boy. Instead, he encouraged Arun to accept his anger and learn to use it wisely.

Gandhi also gave Arun exercises to do, such as keeping a daily journal, in which he listed every act of violence, both active and passive, that he had committed that day. Arun was then able to observe his behavior and work on making positive changes in his life. This kind of powerful teaching is the key to transforming the potentially devastating effects of our dark side.

When we accept our shadow as a natural part of our lives, we can allow it to work for us in positive ways. This is often referred to as "owning" our shadow. It is an essential aspect of self-acceptance and spiritual well-being. Owning our own shadow reflects self-responsibility. It keeps us from projecting our unwanted characteristics onto others and allows us to accept not only our darkest side but also our most brilliant.

Until we learn to accept ourselves fully and unconditionally, we will continue to struggle with bottled-up anger and unrealistic self-expectations, which contribute considerably to the problem of violence in our world. Our work begins when we agree to deal with the warring factions within our own consciousness and embrace ourselves in our entirety.

We Are More than What We Do

There is a big difference between what we *do* and who we *are*. What we accomplish at any given time is based on experience, practice, skill level, environment, opportunity, and a number of other variables. Who we are, on the other hand, is spiritual and enduring.

Each individual is a part of this beautiful mystery we call life. We did not create ourselves, and even though we cannot fully explain how life began, we know that the universal creative force is much larger and more powerful than we can ever imagine. Life exists in so many forms and shapes and thrives even in the most challenging of circumstances. Each of us has been given the gift of life, and we are all worthy of that gift—not because of our wealth or accomplishments but because we exist. We are worthy of being loved because of who we are, not because of who we impress.

The Story of a Perfectionist

There was a time when I believed that my goal in life was to accomplish all my tasks perfectly or risk being rejected by others. I refused to accept my flaws or failings, because I associated them with unworthiness and felt humiliated if I underachieved, no matter what the reason.

I think I knew at a deep level that my mind-set was not really healthy, but I constantly felt compelled to be the best. If someone in my class at school got an A, I had to get an A+. If someone my age received a special award, I had to receive a bigger award. When I was not recognized as the best or when my efforts failed, I berated myself mercilessly and felt undeserving of being loved or comforted. I would mope in my room for days and be unresponsive to others. I felt helpless and hopeless.

Conversely, when I did accomplish my goals in accordance with my ultra-high standards, nothing could get me down. At those victorious times, I felt valuable, lovable, and beautiful. I would bubble over with enthusiasm and looked forward to spending time with others. I felt as if I were on top of the world and nothing bad could touch me.

It goes without saying that during those years I was on an emotional roller coaster where, depending on how well I performed, I either loved myself or hated myself.

In addition to the pressures I put on myself to succeed in my work, I also felt it was necessary to gain the personal approval of others. I would pay close attention to which character traits people admired most and strive to make them my own so that I could be accepted into their circle of friends. I saw that people were attracted to winners, and I desperately wanted to be a winner.

I became defensive whenever anyone criticized me and was often angry with myself for not living up to my own standards of excellence. I was also angry with those around me for letting me down and not living up to my expectations of them. Mostly I was angry because, in my mind, no matter how hard I worked, I couldn't seem to reach a place where anything I did was enough to make me feel good about myself.

Eventually I came to see that my relentless need to seek approval by trying to be successful was rooted in false assumptions, which were contributing in a significant way to my feelings of shame and unworthiness.

As I look back now, I realize that I have accomplished a great deal in my life thus far. I am very grateful for the opportunities I have been given in both of my careers and for those who believed in me and continued to support my efforts, even though things didn't always seem hopeful.

I am also grateful for my failures, because within each failed attempt to accomplish a goal, I was blessed with invaluable lessons for growth that might not have occurred any other way. It has been said that our failures often teach us more than our successes. I believe this is true. Lifting ourselves out of defeat and staying true to our deepest values in spite of the challenges is the archetype of the hero's journey, and we can be grateful that there is a hero within each of us.

During my early years, however, I don't remember being grateful for very much, because I felt I had too much to prove. I continued to strive and push myself toward the next goal, the next opportunity to make myself worthy. I couldn't figure out that what I really needed was to separate who I *was* from what I *did*. In my mind there was no difference. My work was my life and my life was my work. If my work was good, then I was good. If my work was bad, then I was bad. This self-defeating mind-set prevented me from accepting myself, because I really didn't know who I was outside of my work.

Fortunately, along the way I met some brilliant and enlightened teachers, who helped me awaken to the realization that the most important changes I needed to make were not to myself but to the way I *saw* myself. They encouraged me to take another, more compassionate, path to self-acceptance and inner peace.

The first lesson they taught me was that, even though I am not flawless, I am worthy of being loved, because my life, along with all other life, is sacred. These spiritual teachers emphasized that this kind of love, referred to by Gandhi as *ahimsa,* is unconditional and universal. It is not affected by anything we say or do. In Western culture, more familiar terms for this level of love are *divine* love or *agape* love. We will elaborate on the concept of ahimsa in a subsequent chapter.

I began to read books written by great mystics of all faiths, who emphasized the difference between what we do and who we are. Their teachings helped me understand that our achievements, no matter how outstanding, don't make us more lovable; they make us more *accomplished.* These accomplishments alone, as powerful and important as they might be, don't automatically provide us with a sense of self-acceptance and well-being.

Our accomplishments can provide us with wealth and other forms of material security that can make our lives more comfortable. They can also add to our self-confidence, which helps us know that we are capable of fulfilling our tasks. Most importantly, if our accomplishments, whether large or small, contribute in any way toward the betterment of at least one person, we can consider ourselves successful in life.

It is part of our nature to strive for excellence and feel good about our accomplishments. Each of us has a built-in creative mechanism, which gives us the desire as well as the capabilities to fulfill our innate potential. Within each of us is also a desire to give to others and contribute our talents to making a better world.

However, our ambitions to accomplish our goals must be tempered by a healthy belief that we have value beyond that which we are able to accomplish. In other words, our successes in life will contribute to a sense of *self-confidence* (how well we do things), while *self-acceptance* (a nonviolent, noncompetitive state of mind) is unconditional and spiritual in nature; through practice, it will lead us to the understanding and acceptance of others.

This aspect of my spiritual journey has taken me to a place in consciousness where I am better able to experience unity within myself, both the darkness and the light, and to realize that I am acceptable just the way I am. I can stop trying so hard to be good enough (we are already good by nature) and instead work on discovering and developing the enormous power for good that is my divine potential.

Reflections

I am learning to be more conscious of not judging my worth by how much I accomplish. I am far less competitive and judgmental than I used to be and have become more compassionate and vulnerable with others. I realize that in my lifetime I have failed at many tasks, but this has not made me a failure. I have also experienced many successes, but this has not made me better than anyone else or more worthy of love. All humanity is equal in the eyes of the Divine.

As an evolving peacemaker,

I walk the path of

self-acceptance.

Changing our beliefs involves changing our methods of communication and the ways we educate our children.

Leona Evans

Chapter 13

Social and Emotional Intelligence

One of the most powerful forces for positive change in our world is education. Now more than ever there is a growing public demand to enhance the quality of our educational systems, not only by promoting technical skills but by developing ways to enhance life skills as well. These include both personal and interpersonal skills such as self-awareness, compassion for others, nonviolent approaches to problem solving, and other nonacademic methods designed to prepare our young people to engage life more fully and effectively.

Over the past several decades, educators and psychologists have come to realize that including social and emotional development skills as part of children's curriculum adds significantly to the quality of their overall education. It not only contributes to academic success but provides a broader range of skills designed to help students cope with life's challenges in more mature and balanced ways. Terms that are often used to identify this work are *emotional intelligence*, sometimes called *EI*, or *EQ*, (*emotional quotient*), or *SEI* (*social and emotional intelligence*).

As adults we can significantly strengthen our interactions with others by incorporating SEI skills into our daily living. SEI is an aspect of education through which we develop our heart-centered wisdom and combine it with our intellectual capabilities to attain maximum use of our intelligence.

The term emotional intelligence was first used in a 1990 article by Yale researchers Peter Salovey and John. D. Mayer, who defined emotional intelligence as

> The subset of social intelligence that involves the ability to monitor one's own and others' feelings and emotions, to discriminate among them, and to use this information to guide one's thinking and actions.[18]

Since that time, the idea of emotional enrichment as an integral part of education has grown considerably. It has even been lauded as the missing link that can improve the quality of academic education while enhancing character development.

One of the leading-edge thinkers on the subject of expanding education to include human dynamics is Daniel Goleman, author of the 1995 bestseller *Emotional Intelligence: Why It Can Matter More than IQ*. Since that time, dialogue among educators, psychologists and business leaders around the world has expanded rapidly resulting in the development of testing methods to determine levels of EI among those in the workplace. In fact, a number of studies have been conducted in work environments, which reported that there was a significant relationship between EI and effective leadership skills.

In 1993, Daniel Goleman and other researchers developed the Collaborative for Academic, Social, and Emotional Learning (CASEL.org), whose mission is to *ensure that all students become knowledgeable, responsible, caring, and contributing members of society*. The organization also has a research and advisory group dedicated to finding ways to provide ideal learning environments for students.

Social and emotional intelligence includes our capacity to identify and manage our own feelings. It involves being able to empathize with the feelings of others and gain greater social awareness within our personal and professional relationships. SEI also increases our

---

[18]   Peter Salovey and John D. Mayer, *Emotional Intelligence*, (Amityville, NYBaywood Publishing Co., Inc. 1990) 188.

ability to monitor our emotions effectively and apply them to tasks such as thinking and problem solving. In addition, it also helps us understand how to control our impulses and resolve interpersonal conflicts.

The goal of SEI is to develop competence in the areas of self-awareness, self-management, social awareness, relationship skills, and responsible decision making.

The emphasis on social and emotional intelligence in no way diminishes the value of educating the intellect. Instead, it adds a much needed and often neglected dimension to our traditional methods of education. By combining the intellectual and emotional components of the human mind, we become able to educate the whole person.

There are some differences of opinion among psychologists and educators regarding how to accurately assess levels of social and emotional intelligence. However, most agree that developing these skills can create a significant improvement in the quality of our lives and enhance our ability to interact with others in respectful and nonviolent ways. Some of the qualities associated with a high SEI include the following:

- **Self-awareness and self-management.** Accurately assessing our feelings and values, having a healthy sense of self-confidence, expressing our emotions appropriately, setting and working toward meaningful goals, learning to identify and manage our stress, doing our best to make wise and healthy decisions

- **Willingness to hear what others are saying.** Giving people our full attention when they speak, not multitasking or letting our minds wander, being present and attentive

- **Allowing others to speak their minds.** Not interrupting or cutting people off because we think our ideas are more important, giving others the same respect we would wish for ourselves

- **Being open to criticism.** Listening carefully and objectively to criticism without taking it personally or feeling attacked, allowing others to have their point of view, accepting input that can be helpful to us and releasing the rest

- **Seeing things from another's point of view.** Practicing empathy, being open to learning why others feel and act the way they do, allowing ourselves to step into their shoes

- **Taking responsibility for our feelings.** Choosing not to blame others for the way we feel, realizing that our responses to what others say or do are always in our hands

- **Developing relationship skills.** Learning to cooperate with others, managing and resolving interpersonal conflict, asking for help when it is needed

- **Being flexible and open to change.** Understanding that there is more than one right way to do things, being willing to explore options and consider alternatives

- **Having a healthy sense of humor.** Being willing to laugh at some of our own mistakes and avoid taking ourselves too seriously, looking at the bright side of situations

- **Managing our impulses.** Controlling our tempers, refusing to act out of anger, handling stressful situations in rational and nonviolent ways

- **Developing effective negotiating skills.** Working in cooperation with others, respecting their points of view as well as our own, practicing the art of successful compromise

These behaviors let others know that we value their right to express themselves. They also demonstrate a willingness to learn another's point of view without insisting that our opinions are worth more than theirs. In this way we practice respect and compassion for those around us.

Gandhi on the Concept of Education

Gandhi believed strongly that education should include character development. He was against any educational system that only benefitted the intellect. In fact, he felt that knowledge without morality could be dangerous. He believed that effective education should include an integrated approach to producing learned minds and enlightened souls.

Gandhi found the Montessori method of early childhood education to be highly compatible with his own views. Both Gandhi and innovative educator Dr. Maria Montessori (1870-1952) agreed that holistic methods of teaching would contribute greatly toward developing a culture of peace. They advocated early childhood education of the soul based upon respect and compassion for all life. This included developing the skills and values to participate meaningfully in our culturally diverse society. They also shared the belief that a child already possesses these qualities and that learning happens when we create the appropriate conditions for bringing forth the child's potential.

Gandhi became acquainted with the Montessori method when he returned to India in 1915 and saw a small school being administered under her name. He then learned of more such schools in India. However, since there were few volunteers and fewer resources to fund the schools at that time, the work in India did not progress significantly.

by Leona Evans

In 1931, Maria Montessori invited Gandhi to speak at her training institute in London. She then traveled to India in 1939 with her son, Mario, where they stayed until 1945. During those years she trained many teachers in the Montessori method. Today Montessori schools can be found throughout India.

The North American Montessori Teachers' Association estimates that there are about forty-five hundred Montessori schools in the United States and approximately twenty thousand schools around the world. Many other public and private schools have adopted Montessori methods, and there is a growing interest among educators to create advanced teaching methods designed to develop compassionate and self-reliant adults.

Matthew's Montessori Memories

I am very fortunate to have been given early access to an education that focused on developing the whole person. From the age of three through kindergarten I attended the Montessori School at Unity in San Luis Obispo, where my mom is the minister. Ours is a preschool, so when it was time for me to enter the first grade, I transferred to another Montessori school in the area that offered classes through sixth grade. Both schools offered me an amazing education, in which I was taught at a very young age to honor and respect all life.

I can remember my teachers telling us that all people were beautiful in their own way. They said that no matter where we came from, what we looked like, or how we worshipped, we were all equal and deserving of love and respect.

One of the times we honored diversity was on the day before our Thanksgiving holidays. All the children and their families would bring favorite foods from their individual ethnic backgrounds for a big potluck. It was so much fun to taste the different foods and hear everyone's special stories. We all celebrated each other as members of the universal human family.

In preschool our teacher would often start the day by reading a story to us and then asking questions about what she'd read. She encouraged us to speak our minds without ridiculing anyone else's point of view. I felt safe to express myself.

By the time we got to kindergarten, we were learning to read, write, and do our math studies. In addition, we sang, danced, did art projects, and learned to play small instruments. We also had plenty of outdoor time to play games and interact with our friends.

When conflicts took place, my teachers looked for compassionate ways to help solve our issues. Instead of being sent to a principal's office and being lectured or "scared straight," each child involved in the conflict would meet together in the Peace Garden, which was an area at the end of our playground. It was a calm and quiet place with shade trees and several benches. First, each of us would take a turn sharing our feelings and telling his or her side of what had happened. Our teacher would act as mediator and patiently guide us through a process of conflict resolution, with an emphasis on nonviolence. At the end of the discussion she would give us advice on ways to interact more effectively in the future.

As I entered the first grade, I was really happy when I found out that we could choose to do independent "research projects" in the afternoons. First each of us would search our school library and find a topic that we wanted to learn more about. Then we would discuss our ideas with a teacher. We would agree on a completion date, and the teacher would provide us with instructions on where to find the materials we needed. Our projects could be anything from constructing a dinosaur out of reusable materials to drawing a rainforest, or even making a short film on a camcorder. We worked independently and at our own pace. When our projects were finished, we were always proud that we had accomplished something on our own and looked forward to seeing what our classmates had done.

Throughout the year, our teachers would invite different experts to show us local wildlife from animal rescues or we would go on field trips to learn more about our natural world. We were often reminded about the importance of respecting our planet. In fact, one day our teachers invited sanitation experts to teach us the types of plastics that could be recycled and helped us set up a composting bin to eliminate food waste.

We were also responsible for keeping our personal environment neat and clean. At the end of each day we would sweep and clean our work areas so that everything we had used was put back in its place.

From time to time we worked with a dance instructor, who gave us exercises to help us feel grounded and connected to our bodies. We did improvisational movements and learned about deep breathing and relaxation techniques.

I spent five years in the Montessori environment and then enrolled in an online school so that I could pursue my acting career. The online school worked with a number of professional children and teens from all over the world. Their philosophy was similar to the Montessori system. I came away with a great education on a variety of subjects and became a member of the National Honor Society.

I also want to add that my environment at home and at Unity totally affirmed what I was learning at school. I am really grateful to my mom and family for their support.

Even though I've had all these wonderful opportunities, it doesn't mean that I don't have any problems. I still have my down times and angry feelings. I'm a human being, and just like everyone else, I will always be growing and learning. The important thing is that I am able go back to what I have always been taught, and find a way back to love.

Matthew

Healing Our Emotional Baggage

SEI is an educational process designed to help people live well-balanced lives. It honors the wisdom inherent in our feeling nature and provides us with powerful opportunities to develop deeper levels of emotional maturity. This includes being able to identify and heal limiting beliefs from our past that have contributed to shaping our current worldview. As we become more emotionally mature, we will find ourselves in a more advantageous position to examine certain beliefs about others that we learned as children. We are likely to find that seeing things from a different perspective can lift us from negative biases toward others to new levels of compassion and respect.

Some important questions to ask ourselves are, "Why do I believe the way I do about certain people?" "Who taught me that I needed to hate or fear them?" "Why do I believe these individuals are my enemies?"

Too often we hold on tightly to certain opinions and feel responsible for having to defend them, even though sometimes we really don't know why we do so. Some of these opinions involve specific individuals, while others focus on different cultures or groups of people. Are these beliefs really ours, or did we grow up assuming they were true because those in our immediate environment accepted them as true? How many of these beliefs are life-affirming, and how many of them perpetuate negative stereotypes about others that keep us from relating to them in open and compassionate ways?

When we agree to seek honest answers to these questions, we might discover that even though we are open-minded in many ways there are still some old emotional biases we carry, often unconsciously, toward certain people whose heritage or culture we have profiled or labeled as inferior or dangerous. This is often very hard to admit, because we really don't want to believe that we are capable of harboring such feelings. At these times we need to understand that many of our strongest emotions were developed in our childhood and have been, in many cases, buried so deeply in our psyches that we have not had access to them.

During a simple everyday conversation, for example, someone can say something that triggers an unconscious bias within us (part of our shadow). Suddenly we can find ourselves overreacting to an issue that might not bother us at any other time. Afterward we are often mystified and embarrassed by our outburst of emotions. "I don't know where that came from," we might say. "I just wasn't myself." "I don't know what got into me."

The real issue, of course, is not what got into us but what came out of us. Those feelings were already there, and it is important that we acknowledge them, without shame or blame, and set about the process of releasing them. We have within us all that it takes to heal the past and learn to build a new future.

Reflections

The more we develop our emotional intelligence, the better able we are to discover the real motives behind our behaviors and avoid taking actions for the wrong reasons, such as wanting to "get even" with someone. This temptation can be very strong at times but is never the highest choice. We need to develop our impulse control so that rather than acting too quickly or from a place of anger we consciously move in the interest of harmony and justice for all concerned.

As evolving peacemakers, we are called upon to develop the wisest and most appropriate ways of clearing our minds of any hidden resentments and establishing respectful and authentic relationships. This is a process that involves attention, practice, and a willingness to understand the power of forgiveness.

As an evolving peacemaker,

I walk the path of

emotional intelligence.

Chapter 14

With Malice toward None

Great thinkers throughout the ages have made exhaustive efforts to identify the human condition. What is the nature of humanity? Why is there evil in the world? Certain theologians have concluded that humanity is inherently evil and needs to be saved. Other mystics have determined that humankind is inherently good and that evil in the world stems from ignorance of our true nature. From this perspective, humanity does not need to be *saved* but needs to *awaken* to the potential for goodness that is already within us.

Gandhi believed that humanity is not inherently evil and that the goodness and beauty we seek are already part of our nature. The One Power has created each of us in truth and in love. What, then, is the nature of evil? In his book *The Way to God*, Gandhi reveals that while he acknowledges the existence of evil, he does not claim to explain it rationally. He does believe, however, that humanity is essentially good and has the innate power to awaken to its true nature:

> We are of God, even as a little drop of water is of the ocean. Imagine it torn away from the ocean and flung millions of miles away. It becomes helpless, torn from its surroundings, and cannot feel the might and majesty of the ocean. But if someone could point out to it that it is the ocean, its faith

would revive, it would dance with joy and the whole of the might and majesty of the ocean would be reflected in it.[19]

Arun Gandhi confirmed that his grandfather believed that God exists in every human being. He also believed that heaven and hell are here on earth and that we create our own heaven and hell by the choices we make.

If we behave properly, if we have love and respect for all humanity, then we are creating a heavenly atmosphere around us. But if we are filled with hate and prejudice and anger and we reflect that in our relationships with others we are creating hell for ourselves." [20] Arun Gandhi

One of the most painful ways we create hell on earth in our personal lives is by holding onto grudges and resentments toward others who have harmed us. When we habitually relive abusive experiences in our minds, we unwittingly place ourselves in an emotional prison where we suffer the same abuses over and over again.

On a global level, we experience hell when we see various forms of terrorism and bigotry taking place throughout the world on a regular basis. How do we stay balanced in the face of so much turmoil? How can we keep from feeling so enraged by our culture of violence that we begin to see enemies all around us and take the wrong kind of action out of anger or pent-up frustration?

Who is Our Enemy?

If we take a close look at the history of war, we will find that throughout the years certain people in power have repeatedly used

---

[19] Mahatma Gandhi, *The Way to God*, (Berkeley, CA, Berkeley Hills Books, 1999) 40.

[20] Matthew J. Evans, *A Quest For Peace: Nonviolence Among Religions* (WGIFilms, 2012)

strategies, subtly or not so subtly, to target various ethnicities, cultures, or religions and turn them into scapegoats for political and economic gain. Things are not always what they seem, and we can't always believe what we hear, especially when the subject matter involves accusations against entire groups of people.

Every form of prejudice provides ample fuel for the perpetuation of hell on earth, and we want to be clear within our souls that we are not inadvertently supporting any of these ideologies by our action or inaction.

As evolving peacemakers we must stay aware of what is going on in the world and make every effort to hear all sides of a situation before taking action. When we do decide to move forward, we need to be certain that our activities are based on rational thinking and nonviolent principles. We never want to take action for the sake of revenge, which many mistakenly refer to as justice. Instead, we want to focus our attention on the goal of true fairness and equality for all.

Most importantly, we always need to keep in mind that we are not separate from one another. What we do to anyone else we also do to ourselves. This realization lays the groundwork for creative changes to occur in our relations with one another.

Hundreds of books and articles have been published on the art of forgiveness. The concept itself, however, still seems to be abstract, and a large segment of our population finds it difficult to put into practice. This is due in large part to the popular, but severely flawed, eye-for-an-eye thinking. As long as we believe we must render payback or get even with another before we can forgive them, we miss the point entirely.

Too often we hold onto our resentments, because we want to be certain that justice is being served. We convince ourselves that the only way to accomplish this goal is by keeping our anger alive until the others pay for what they did. Of course there is a huge price to pay for keeping our anger alive, and we are the ones who pay it. Living with thoughts of revenge on a daily basis not only increases our pent-up anger but severely diminishes our vitality and capacity for happiness. Our misguided attempts to punish others cause us to punish ourselves over and over again.

On the other end of the spectrum, we can be so fearful of confronting our anger that we try to make our feelings go away by pretending the situation never happened. Obviously, this is only a temporary solution and does not further the process of genuine forgiveness. Denying our own reality is self-defeating and ends up becoming fuel for the shadow side of our consciousness. Remember that our pent-up anger does not go away, it just collects underneath the surface of our minds until it explodes when we least expect it.

What Forgiveness is Not

Contrary to popular belief, forgiveness is not minimizing, excusing, or condoning the action that occurred. It is not denying our pain or pretending that nothing happened. In fact, trying too hard to diminish or deny what happened actually contributes to the buildup of resentment within us. This is because, without realizing it, we are confirming that our feelings don't matter. Before we can practice true forgiveness, we need to make sure that we stop disrespecting, demeaning, or ignoring our own truths.

Continuing to live in an abusive environment is not forgiveness either. If we are being mistreated on a regular basis and believe we are practicing forgiveness by choosing to remain in the situation, we give the abuser permission to go on mistreating us. This is a type of martyrdom generated by fear and a lack of self-worth, which causes harm not only to ourselves but to our children as well.

No one deserves to live in an atmosphere of abuse. It is a worldwide problem that affects more individuals than we might expect. In some situations people can find the inner strength to liberate themselves from a cycle of abuse. In other cases they require help. Fortunately, lawmakers, humanitarian organizations, and private citizens have been working to find ways of alleviating all types of abuse that affect children, spouses, the elderly, and women. They work diligently to provide legal assistance, educational resources, and encouragement to victims. It is a work in progress that still has a long way to go, but it is a work that many of us can find ways to support.

It might surprise us to learn that forgiveness does not require us to stay friends with those whom we have forgiven. Although we must love them, it is not always in our best interests to become actively involved with them again.

When I was a child, we were encouraged to shake hands and be friends whenever we had an argument with our playmates. We were taught that it was important to behave as though the altercation had never taken place. We seldom, if ever, discussed the reason for our arguments. It was just assumed that whatever had caused the disagreement would disappear if we stopped talking about it.

When I grew older, I realized that relationships are not always so simple. Regardless of our efforts to maintain a personal connection with someone who has harmed us, or whom we have harmed, there are times when it is not possible to do so. Ours is a world of diversity, in which we find all manner of opinions, ideas, and points of view. If another refuses to forgive us, all we can do is bless them and let them go.

Unfortunately, we know too well that there are those for whom the goal is eliminating differences rather than learning to live with them. It is not always possible to befriend the individuals in such cases. However, it is most important that we love them. We do this not on the basis of what they have done but because holding onto painful grudges diminishes all of us and perpetuates a culture of violence.

Forgiveness Defined

True forgiveness can be defined as acceptance without prejudice. It is our ability to make peace with what we really wanted but didn't get from others. This includes all types of situations, ranging from not getting the love we wanted as children to being abused, cheated, lied to, or oppressed as adults. Forgiving others means that we no longer identify ourselves by these experiences or allow them to overtake our lives. It means we are coming to peace with what is.

We all have instances in our lives when our expectations have not been met. Whether or not all these expectations were reasonable is not the point. We have all suffered disappointment, rejection, and anger when others have denied our needs and desires. While it is important that we feel our feelings and process these situations, there comes a time when dwelling on them and identifying with them becomes detrimental to our health and our capacity to function in healthy ways.

Forgiveness is about having the inner resolve to release our thoughts of avenging those who have harmed us, whether we believe they deserve it or not. It begins by understanding that we are more valuable than the way others have defined us. We are stronger than the challenging circumstances of our past and more resilient to all of the times we didn't get what we wanted. As we internalize these ideas, we will find the inner strength to start releasing our resentments and free ourselves from the pain of our past.

- Forgiveness is letting go of the anger we have inadvertently allowed to poison our souls.

- Forgiveness is giving up our need to even the score with those who have wounded us.

- Forgiveness is healing past wounds so that we don't project our fears and mistrust onto our current relationships and perceive insults when none were intended.

- Forgiveness is extending compassion to those who have harmed us.

Remember, no matter how challenging our forgiveness work appears to be, it is not nearly as difficult as carrying an overflow of unresolved grievances and giving them permission to contaminate the quality of our lives.

Agreeing to Disagree

Even though there are times when we cannot resolve our differences with others, we always have the option to "agree to disagree." This is when we each allow the other to have his or her own opinions and concur that what we have in common is greater and more enduring than our differences.

Is there really a way to agree to disagree? Absolutely! It is very possible to disagree passionately with others, as long as we understand that our way isn't the only way. On the subject of religion, for example, we can be devoted to our particular beliefs and find great comfort in following the tenets of our specific faith. However, this does not mean we must require others to find spiritual comfort in the same way. In the best of circumstances, we will discuss our differing views and learn about one another's beliefs without feeling a need to prove we are right. This does not make either of us wrong, it just means we don't agree. If we can leave it at that, there is no need to forgive anything.

Unfortunately, most people are not trained in the art of constructive discourse, and too often the disagreement becomes personal. For instance, if we find ourselves discussing a sensitive topic with someone whose philosophy is different from our own, it is only natural for both of us to defend our particular points of view. This can make for a stimulating and interesting ideological discussion—until we start feeling personally attacked. That is where we get off the track.

As soon as the discussion moves from the level of ideas to the level of personalities, it deteriorates into a power struggle. Before we know it, our interesting philosophical exchange becomes combative and begins to involve personal insults and name-calling. The struggle to force others to see things our way often ends badly for all participants and can create resentments that are difficult to forgive.

Conversely, the process of agreeing to disagree does not involve force or passive violence. It is an objective and reasonable exchange of ideas that occurs when individuals have opposing points of view. The goal is to be able to disagree with one another and not feel personally diminished or defeated just because we have not convinced the other that our way is right.

In situations when it is necessary to come to a single decision, we can still keep the dialogue focused on the issues without becoming defensive or engaging in a battle of wills. As we relinquish our need to score a personal victory and work toward a logical and compassionate solution to our problems, we will find no animosity and nothing to forgive. In fact, our attitude of nonresistance can actually open a way for creative solutions we hadn't thought of before.

As we have discussed in previous chapters, nonviolent communication requires that we practice new ways of thinking and engage in more effective ways of communication. The more we practice tolerance and acceptance, the better able we are to engage in respectful interaction with others. This is a process that involves repetition, patience, and a willingness to be content with small victories.

The aim of forgiveness, then, is not to erase the past or try to rewrite history. Real forgiveness occurs when we heal our resentments, learn everything we can from our experiences, and practice love in spite of everything that has taken place.

As an evolving peacemaker,

I walk the path of

Forgiving others.

All true forgiveness involves self-forgiveness. When we can accept responsibility for our own actions and become willing to work toward healing ourselves, it is possible to find redemption in the most unlikely places.

Leona Evans

Chapter 15

The Forgiving Power of Love

Those who are raised in an atmosphere of violence often learn that one is either a victim or a victimizer. They are taught that the only way to survive is to become a victimizer. In this kill-or-be-killed atmosphere, many of those who manage to stay alive end up in prison. Too often they become repeat offenders, because they don't let go of the old beliefs that brought them there in the first place. They have been taught that there are enemies all around them and that if they trust anyone outside their immediate environment, or try to make peace with their rivals, it can mean death to them and their families. This is a cycle of violence based on an eye-for-an-eye mentality, which continues to destroy people of all ages and cultures.

Fortunately, there are others who are working diligently to plant seeds of nonviolence so as to make a positive difference in peoples' lives. Many have been successful in reaching those who are ready to learn new ways of living.

In 2011 my son, Matthew, produced a documentary short film called *Poetic Justice Project*, which won the 2014 Gold Jury Prize Youth Visions at the Social Justice Film Festival in Seattle. Poetic Justice Project is a nonprofit program based in Santa Maria, California, which has as its mission the advancement of social justice by engaging formerly incarcerated people in original theater examining crime, punishment, and redemption.

Founding Artistic Director Deborah Tobola taught creative writing and theater in California prisons for more than twelve years. She saw the need for an arts reentry program and retired from the California Department of Corrections and Rehabilitation to begin Poetic Justice Project in 2009. Since that time, Poetic Justice Project has involved close to one hundred formerly incarcerated youth and adults in fifteen theatrical productions designed to unlock hearts and minds through theater and the arts.

While Matthew was filming *Poetic Justice Project,* we had the occasion to meet and become friends with an extraordinary member of the group named Willie Bermudez. Both Matthew and I were deeply moved by his struggles, his redemption, and the series of events that provided him with a powerful opportunity to forgive himself.

Willie's Story

Willie Bermudez was incarcerated for thirty-eight years of his life, from Youth Authority, where he served time for battery on an officer, to several high-security prisons, where he was held for assaulting an inmate and killing another.

Willie was eventually transferred to a California prison, where he participated in the Arts in Corrections Program and met Deborah Tobola. During his years in prison, Willie spent time developing his talent for painting and became an accomplished artist. Through his association with Ms. Tobola he discovered his talent for acting and became involved in the work of Poetic Justice Project. Today he serves as a member of their advisory board.

Matthew and I recently contacted Willie and asked for his input on the topic of forgiveness. He was more than willing to share the circumstances through which he came to forgive himself and revealed the process that lifted him from his burden of guilt.

Willie was born in 1950 and grew up in a family who believed, as many did, that if parents spared the rod they would spoil the child. Concerned that his son would end up in bad company, Willie's father regularly spanked him or beat him as punishment for misbehaving. However, instead of learning to obey the rules, Willie learned that the one who hits the hardest has the power.

By the time Willie reached his teen years, he started rebelling against his parents and began hanging out with a group of other rebellious teens. He looked up to the older crowd because they were streetwise and fearless. Willie wanted to be tough and cool.

Before long Willie was getting arrested for drug use. He never took those arrests seriously, because the outcome was always the same. He would spend a short time in jail, be released, and then go out and do drugs again. Willie commented, "I had no respect for myself or other people. I did drugs and hung around with a bad crowd. I thought that being a crazy dude would make me a hero."

In 1970, things changed for Willie. This time he was arrested for battery on a police officer and was remanded to Youth Authority. During his time there, Willie was involved in a fight and sent to a facility that was populated by both youth and adult inmates. It was there that Willie was reunited with some of his old crowd and started to hang out with a gang.

Prison gangs are notoriously ruthless. If the members feel they have been insulted or demeaned in any way, they will be quick to retaliate against their offender. One day, after a particularly antagonistic encounter with another inmate, Willie's gang decided to take revenge. They arranged for a knife to be smuggled into the prison and Willie, always wanting to be the tough one, volunteered to stab the inmate.

The next day Willie woke up to find that he had become a hero among his fellow prisoners. He was congratulated and slapped on the back for his loyalty and fearlessness. After that he became an official gang member and regularly engaged in various forms of violence. These acts of violence escalated, until one day in 1975 Willie ended up killing a fellow inmate. For this crime he received a life sentence and was placed in maximum security.

The Road Back

During the following years, Willie spent a great deal of his time alone. He spent much of the day doing pencil drawings and discovered he had a real talent for fine art. One day someone suggested that if Willie could learn to draw pictures of ballerinas he could probably sell them and make good money. Willie liked the idea and wrote to several dance studios asking for magazine photos of professional dancers at work. In time a studio owner responded to his request. Gradually they began a correspondence, which led to a spiritually based friendship that continues to this day. Willie calls her "Sis."

At the beginning of their correspondence in 1979, Sis was interested in hearing Willie's story. As they continued to exchange letters, she became more and more impressed with his insightful responses to her questions. She came to see a wisdom and goodness within him that he had not been able to see in himself. Her faith in Willie inspired him to want to learn more about his inner potential. Soon he began reading books on spirituality and the power of the mind.

The more Willie read, the more he started questioning himself, "Why do I admire the gang mentality?" "Why do I leave my destiny in the hands of other criminals?" "Who is the real me?"

In 1986, after a great deal of journaling and intense self-examination, Willie made a life-altering decision to quit the prison gang. He knew that any gang member who chose to quit took the risk of being murdered by the other members. Even so, Willie decided that he would rather die in the prison yard than continue to participate in the violent gang activities.

When the gang learned of Willie's decision to quit, they attempted to kill him by slashing his throat. The guards immediately rushed Willie to the prison hospital, where he eventually recovered from his injuries. He was then transferred to another facility.

As the years passed, Willie continued to study spiritual and self-help materials and made significant changes in his attitude and behavior. After a time, Willie was relocated to another prison, where he took art classes and participated in workshops designed to help improve the quality of his life

Finding Forgiveness

One weekend Willie took part in a workshop sponsored by an organization aimed at providing alternatives to violence. One of the goals of the workshop was to help ease racial tension among the inmates.

During a community-building exercise, the inmates were asked to place their chairs in two circles, one inside the other. The chairs of the inner circle were positioned outward so that the inmates were able to face each other. The facilitator emphasized that despite the widespread racial divide that created violence among individual gangs, they actually had a great deal in common. They were all doing time in prison, they all had people on the outside who loved them, they were all going through similar struggles, etc. At one point she asked the inmates to take several moments to look at one other and make an effort to recognize the humanity in every face.

As the exercise progressed, Willie found himself looking into the eyes of the facilitator. He remembered that during her introduction she had shared that her son had been killed in a robbery. Willie thought, *Any one of my fellow inmates sitting in these circles could have been responsible for her son's death. Yet here she is reaching out to every one of us in love, doing all she can do to help us improve ourselves. She has forgiven us.*

After a few moments, Willie had another insight: *This woman could have been the mother of the man I killed. Even so, she has already forgiven me.*

Finally Willie realized, *This woman could be my own mother, who has endured great suffering because of my actions. Yet she has forgiven me.*

Suddenly Willie was filled with an overwhelming rush of empathy and compassion. It was both deeply painful and exhilarating at the same time.

In that moment he understood: *If I have already been forgiven, I can now forgive myself.*

As Willie shared this story with Matthew and me, he broke down and sobbed. He recalled the many years of self-hatred and remorse that had dominated his life. He also remembered, with tremendous gratitude, that special weekend workshop when he had opened his heart and given himself permission to love.

Willie was released from prison in 2008. A year later he contacted Deborah Tobola and became involved with Poetic Justice Project. Today Willie paints, acts, practices his spirituality, and lectures on redemption through the arts. He also volunteers his time in service to others. He has become a beautiful example of love in action.

Matthew, Willie Bermudez, and Leona (2016)

I spoke to Willie on the phone recently and thanked him again for giving us permission to share his powerful and inspiring story.

He told us that by sharing his experiences he hoped to help others see that it is never too late to begin again.

Toward the end of our conversation Willie said, "Everybody is part of one community. Life is supposed to be about loving everyone."

Forgiving through the Power of Love

Gandhi referred to the highest form of love as *ahimsa*, which is an identification with and love for all living things.

Ahimsa is a transcendent form of love that lifts us from the level of personal bias to one of unconditional acceptance and desire for the other's well-being. It is a spiritual love that is powerful enough to heal even the most painful wounds. "Love of the hater is the most difficult of all. But by the grace of God even this most difficult thing becomes easy to accomplish if we want to do it." [21]

Ahimsa is the foundation of Gandhi's philosophy of nonviolence. He believed this quality is inherent in the soul of all humanity and that the practice of ahimsa is the means to truth (satyagraha). There is no real forgiveness without it. Willie's story confirms this.

---

[21]   Richard Attenborough, *The Words of Gandhi (William Morrow, 2001)*

As an evolving peacemaker,

I walk the path of

Self-Forgiveness

True love is boundless like the ocean and swelling within one, spreads itself out and crossing all boundaries and frontiers, envelops the whole world.[22]

Gandhi

---

[22] Mahatma Gandhi, *The Way to God*, (Berkeley CA.Berkeley Hills Books,1999), 55.

Chapter 16

Ahimsa: Heaven on Earth

A himsa is derived from a Sanskrit term inspired by the premise that all life is sacred and contains the spark of universal divine energy. Therefore, to inflict harm upon another is the same as inflicting harm upon oneself. Gandhi explains, "True ahimsa should mean a complete freedom from ill-will, anger and hate and an overflowing love for all."[23]

The term ahimsa is often understood as the avoidance of physical force. Gandhi felt this definition didn't fully encompass the essential meaning of the idea. He believed that ahimsa is an active force of the highest order. "Ahimsa does not simply mean non-killing. It means not to injure any creature by thought, word, or deed ... Ahimsa is the attribute of the soul and therefore to be practiced by everybody in all the affairs of life."[24]

Gandhi understood ahimsa as a creative energy force that embodies the highest forms of love and compassion and is at the foundation of all religions. He understood this force to be inherent in all life and that by calling it forth from inside our souls we lift ourselves to a level of unconditional love and acceptance of everyone. Ahimsa was at the foundation of Gandhi's search for truth.

---

[23] D. G. Tendulkar, *Mahatma*, Volume 11, (Ministry of Information, 1928), 418–420.

[24] Ibid

While Gandhi felt it was appropriate to criticize or attack a system, he never believed in criticizing or attacking an individual. He understood that all were created by the same God and possessed the same divine attributes. To debase even one individual would be the same as hurting oneself. For this reason, Gandhi worked tirelessly to remove the stigma of the "untouchables" in India.

Untouchables is the former name for any member of a Hindu group outside the caste system. In 1949 the use of the term *untouchable* was declared unconstitutional. However, for many years the untouchables were subjected to degrading social restrictions. They were forbidden to enter schools or temples or drink water from the same wells as the rest of the population. Their very presence was thought to be visually contaminating to others. Gandhi worked ceaselessly to remove the stigma from these individuals, whom he called "children of God." Gandhi often said that he was "touchable by birth but untouchable by choice." This was one of the ways he practiced ahimsa.

Gandhi also believed that an essential aspect of ahimsa is giving of ourselves in loving service to others. He advised that whenever we find ourselves at a crossroads in life and are doubtful as to which course of action to pursue, we should take a moment and call to mind the poorest and weakest person we have ever seen. Then we are to ask ourselves if the action we contemplate will be of any benefit to that person. Will that person be better off in any way? Will we be engaging in any sort of service that could make a positive difference in that person's life, even at the smallest level? Gandhi concluded that when we receive the answers to those questions, all indecision melts away in the light of greater clarity and compassion.

For Gandhi, ahimsa was not a cloistered virtue but a rule of conduct for society; it included thoughts and words as well as action. He believed we must apply the principles of nonviolence and loving-kindness to every area of our lives. He acknowledged that this practice was by no means easy. It requires constant vigilance, along with a dedication to demonstrating the highest qualities within ourselves, even in the face of extreme adversity. Gandhi was willing to give his life for these principles.

From Hatred to Love

In 1946, after the British left India, the country was partitioned into two independent nation-states. The Hindus were to live in India and the Muslims in Pakistan. There was an enormous upheaval as hundreds and thousands of people were forced to vacate the homes that they had occupied for generations. Hindus and Muslims fought one another, and there was much violence and bloodshed. Gandhi was deeply discouraged. For all his efforts to teach the principles of nonviolence, people did not seem to be listening. Even though he was frail and in poor health, Gandhi decided to go on a fast until the people stopped fighting one another. The place he chose was a small hut in a poor Muslim ghetto of Calcutta.

During this time, there was a man named Souren Bannerji who lived in Calcutta with his wife and children. He was regarded by those around him as a peaceful man. In 1946, however, the unthinkable happened. His wife, son, and daughter were brutally raped and murdered by a rage-filled crowd of Muslims. In the midst of his unspeakable grief and anger, Souren joined a violent Hindu mob looking for revenge. He took part in the massacre of a Muslim family.

In an article called "Overcoming Hatred and Revenge through Love," Arun wrote this:

> Having killed a child Souren knew he'd be haunted forever. When he learned of Gandhi's fasting unto death for this violence, he went to him and pleaded for forgiveness. "I have committed a heinous crime. I murdered a Muslim family after my family was killed. My life has become a living hell. I can't accept the additional burden of your death on my conscience. Bapu, please give up your fast." Gandhi replied: "I have a suggestion. First, for yourself, go and find an orphan Muslim baby and nurture the baby as your own. You must allow the baby to grow up in its own faith."

Souren remembered the powerful words Gandhi had spoken to him. As he searched for an orphaned Muslim child, he found a young Muslim woman with her infant son who had miraculously escaped death. After her husband and family were murdered, she had been repeatedly raped and was now an outcast. In a moment of horrific violence, her life had changed forever, just as Souren's had been. As they told each other of their suffering, Souren and Maryam found they had much in common. After a while they developed a relationship with one another.

Arun continued:

One day Souren shared with Maryam the last words he had heard from Gandhi. "We are one human race. Don't let religion divide us." Souren and Maryam were married. In the spirit of Gandhi, they decided they would study both of their religions and absorb the good each had to offer. I met Souren in Bombay several years later. He and Maryam had two children: Maryam's son whom Souren had adopted, and a daughter ... They confided: We understand what Gandhi meant when he said, "Change can come only one life at a time."[25]

The compelling story of Souren and his redemption is a powerful example of how acts of violence performed in the heat of anger destroy innocent lives and bring about devastation for all involved. It also offers hope, as Souren's reaction to his acts of violence and his fear that Gandhi might actually die moved him to seek a way out of his pain and remorse. Gandhi offered Souren the key to redemption by suggesting that he give to one child what he had taken from another. Only then could he open a way to heal the unspeakable pain that consumed him.

Souren found many unexpected blessings as a result of Gandhi's profound advice. He learned the value of forgiveness, and in doing

---

[25]   Arun Gandhi, "Overcoming Hatred and Revenge through Love", (*Fellowship Magazine*, July/August 1998)

so discovered the gift of love where he least expected it. Furthermore, without his ever knowing it, the story of his encounter with Gandhi has become one of the most moving and memorable accounts of redemption in modern history. In fact, it is touchingly recounted in the 1982 Academy Award–winning film *Gandhi*, starring Ben Kingsley and directed by David Attenborough. It will continue to teach future generations that love is the most powerful force in the world.

by Leona Evans

Reflections

The most important lesson we can learn as we pursue the path of the evolving peacemaker is that through love we become able to heal even the deepest of wounds and soar to the greatest heights of loving-kindness.

As we allow our anger and pain to be transformed by the power of love we open ourselves to living our lives in alignment with our highest spiritual potential. This includes having compassion for all life and being willing to see the presence of the divine in every face, including our own.

As an evolving peacemaker,

I walk the path of

love.

We are profoundly interconnected and interrelated. This means that instead of just seeing ourselves as either dependent or independent, we now are called upon to put into practice the idea of interdependence: a state of mutual reliance on one another as kindred spirits. Interdependence has its roots in the concept of the unity of all life.

Leona Evans

Chapter 17

Honoring Our Relationship with All Life

by Matthew J. Evans

We are not independent individuals; we are interdependent, interconnected and interrelated. What happens to us happens to others and what happens to others happens to us, and we have to respect that.[26]

Arun Gandhi

W hen we approach the topic of being aligned with all life, I imagine many people would think this is a metaphor, but it's really a biological reality.

Every living thing on earth is related to all the others through a common ancestor, single-celled organisms.

Imagine the tree of life. On every branch there are families of organisms. On one branch there are plants, trees, and flowers. On another branch there are fish. On still another are reptiles, and so on. Every species is represented on this tree. All the similar organisms are clustered close together on the tree, and those less similar are farther apart. Still, it is one tree. All the branches are held together

---

[26] Matthew J. Evans, *A Quest For Peace: Nonviolence Among Religions* (WGIFilms, 2012)

by the trunk, in which you find the common ancestor: tiny, ancient single-celled organisms.

Going back millions and millions of years, scientists can trace the evolution of life to its beginning with a small group of single-celled organisms that over the years evolved into plants, animals, and diversified into the many and varied species that are alive today. But every organism can be traced back to a common ancestor, illustrating a unity with all life.

As I continued to study more about how we are different but still the same, I came across some important information about races of people. According to the research of the Human Genome Project (1990–2003), the genes that define our physical characteristics are comprised of approximately 0.1 percent of our genetic makeup.[27] This is a very powerful fact when we think of how much racism there is in the world. The truth is that there is only one race—the human race! We have diverse ethnicities, but those differences are cultural, not biological. The *Encyclopaedia Britannica* explains it this way:

> Genetic studies in the late 20th century refuted the existence of biogenetically distinct races and scholars now argue that races are cultural inventions reflecting specific attitudes and beliefs that were imposed on different populations in the wake of western European conquests beginning in the fifteenth century.[28]

This distinction between race and ethnicity is very important, because it is a great example of diversity within unity. Human beings can look, sound, believe, worship, or think differently from one another and still be the same biologically. This is so exciting, because scientific discoveries are supporting our spiritual understanding of the diversity within unity.

---

[27]   (Race in a Genetic World, Harvard Magazine, published May–June 2008, harvardmagazine.com/2008/05/race-in-a-genetic-world-html)

[28]   "Race," Encyclopædia Britannica, accessed May 19, 2016. http://kids.britannica.com/blackhistory/article-9126111

Gandhi states:

> One who looks upon the universe as various facets of God will certainly have the beatific vision. All our knowledge and spiritual exercises are fruitless, so long as we have not had this vision.[29]

So, if we're each genetically related to all life on earth, this includes the stars, the water, the cosmos, and the ground beneath our feet.

One of my favorite phrases that the late astronomer, astrophysicist, and cosmologist Carl Sagan made popular was, "We are all made of star stuff." This means that the same elements of carbon, nitrogen, oxygen, and all the other elements that make up the beautiful stars and nebulae in the night sky are also within us. In fact, of the twenty-seven elements that are commonly found in the human body, all of them are contained within the stars that are burning brightly as we look up into the night sky.

Now that we see a connection with every single piece of matter in our universe, we can understand how important it is to treat each other and our planet with utmost respect.

Respecting Our Planet

Gandhi taught that respect for our natural resources was part of his philosophy of satyagraha. In fact, when twelve-year-old Arun threw away a pencil because he thought it was too short to use anymore, his grandfather made him take a flashlight outside to look for it. When Arun finally found the pencil stub two hours later, Gandhi explained that wasting our precious resources was an example of violence against nature. It was an important lesson for Arun, who is now very active in supporting ways to preserve our natural resources and respect our ecosystem.

---

[29] Mahatma Gandhi, *The Way to God*, (Berkeley, CA, Berkeley Hills Books, 1999), 93.

During Gandhi's time, there were scientists who were beginning to see the dangerous implications of climate change. Very few people paid attention. As the decades went on, more and more people came to understand the seriousness of the situation, and now many are taking action to reverse climate change by doing things to reduce their carbon footprint.

"Reduce, reuse, and recycle" is the famous phrase that reminds us of ways to respect our planet and help mitigate climate change. One of the ways we can reduce waste is by making use of all the food we buy instead of throwing it away. This lowers the amount of food that goes into landfills, helping to prevent excess methane emissions. It also reminds us that we can share our excess food with those who need it.

We can reuse by donating our old goods instead of throwing them away. We can also think of creative ways to turn an item that had a specific use into something else. For example, turning an old wastebasket into a planter or using old boxes and used holiday cards to create storage and decorative works of art. We can even harvest seeds from vegetables such as beans, beets, or broccoli and plant them in a garden.

We can recycle by reclaiming old materials such as wood, glass, and plastic and repurposing them to create new goods. By recycling our old electronics, we can reuse metals that would otherwise need to be collected by strip mining and other wasteful practices.

By purchasing low-emission vehicles and putting solar panels on our roofs, we slowly begin to get away from relying on fossil fuels to power our homes and cities. However, if buying hybrid cars and solar panels might be too expensive, there are still many other ways we can work toward healing our planet. Planting trees can literally scrub the air of the carbon dioxide we produce and, in return, create the oxygen we need to survive.

Everyone can find ways to contribute to the well-being of our planet, and each effort is important. However, there are those who are in a position to make a more sizable impact on our world. One of those people is Robert Redford. I had the amazing opportunity to spend a month on his property in Sundance, Utah, and see some of the results of his humanitarian work.

Working at Sundance

When I was nine years old, I was hired as an actor for the 2006 Sundance Directors Lab sponsored by the Sundance Institute. Eight young directors from around the world got the chance to work with industry legends on how to most effectively direct the films they were currently working on. I worked with a director from New Zealand, and we filmed scenes every day under the guidance of Robert Redford (who asked us to call him Bob, but I was too shy) and other film experts.

Every week a different group of actors, cinematographers, directors, editors, etc. would come to Sundance and take turns working with the directors as they filmed their scenes. I met and learned from some wonderful industry professionals.

One of the most inspiring parts of my time at Sundance was to see firsthand what it means to conserve and respect our natural resources.

Robert Redford has been a passionate environmentalist since the 1970s, and he has worked tirelessly to protect natural habitats around the world. Sundance, Utah, is primarily a resort, but it is much more. Bob said his mission was to develop a little and to preserve a great deal, and Sundance is a perfect example of that.

by Leona Evans

Sundance, Utah, 2006

Over five thousand acres of the resort are set aside as a natural preserve and easement. Sundance purchases wind-produced power, which equals 100 percent of their usage. In fact, the wind power they purchase has the yearly equivalent of planting twelve and a half thousand trees.

The rooms of the resort are cleaned with nontoxic cleaning agents to prevent harmful chemicals spilling into the natural surroundings. In the general store they use recycled and organic materials for their T-shirts, grocery bags, housewares, and even their paper cups and coffee filters. They recycle massive amounts of what they produce, using paper and wood waste to make pens, pencils, and other useful items. In fact, most of the wood used in construction was reclaimed, and the stone was either harvested from the Sundance property or taken from nearby quarries, to have as minimal an impact on the environment as possible.

During my time at Sundance I watched closely as workers made glass art from recycled broken glass in their open-air foundry. I also learned to make jewelry from recycled metals. The glass blowing was amazing to watch and something I'd never seen before. They roll up glowing balls of molten glass on long poles and then blow air through the poles and shape the glass as it cools. The color of the glass slowly becomes visible as it cools from a bright burning orange to green, or blue, or whatever color they want.

The Sundance staff also offers visitors the opportunity to participate in a ride-along with the reserve's rangers and see what it takes to monitor animal populations, prevent illegal hunting, and ensure the safety of visitors and the land itself.

Being at Sundance made me realize that there are so many ways to conserve our resources and that as a society we are only scratching the surface. Sundance focuses on what they can do there, but it really made me wonder what the world would be like if all of us could find our own special ways to make the most of our environment while having as little negative impact as possible.

Robert Redford's work for the environment reaches far beyond Sundance. He has fought for habitats and preserves all over the world. One of his largest victories was his twenty-year battle to stop development of 1.7 million acres of land in Utah.

The Grand Staircase-Escalante National Monument was under threat of development in 1975 when Robert Redford first brought this place to national attention. He continued to fight to keep the land undeveloped, stopping coal mines and other harmful development. In 1996, President Bill Clinton set aside the land as a national monument, protecting it from any human destruction.

Robert Redford has given talks at the United Nations urging world leaders to take action toward improving our environment. He uses his platform as an accomplished actor and Oscar–winning director to make his voice heard. He is a role model to me and I'm sure to many others who are learning how to interact with our environment to promote harmony on our planet.

We can't all speak at the UN, lobby congress or presidents, or build a small town devoted to ecological preservation, but he could and did. I am so proud of his work and grateful to have been part of the Sundance experience.

Just like any of the other concepts in this book, healing our planet can't happen overnight. There are those who are already doing as much as they can to reduce their carbon footprint and educate the public about climate change and responsible ecological practices. However, there are still many people around the world who aren't as knowledgeable in this subject or don't believe that what they do makes a difference. The truth is that everything we do in the interest of protecting and preserving life makes a difference.

The biggest thing I am learning from our environmental activists is that they are teaching through example. They're putting their time, energy, money, and passion into *being* the change they want to see in the world. Their work will continue to inspire me to do my part.

As an evolving peacemaker,

I walk the path of

unity with all life.

Relationships in the philosophy of nonviolence must be built on the four concepts of respect, understanding, acceptance, and appreciation ... We have to respect ourselves and respect each other and respect our connection with all of creation.

Arun Gandhi[30]

---

[30] Matthew J. Evans, *A Quest For Peace: Nonviolence Among Religions* (WGIFilms, 2012)

Chapter 18

Do Unto Others

Generally speaking, most people tend to equate the term *respect* with admiration. For example, one might say, "I respect my father because he has lived a life of integrity" or "I respect my teacher because of the inspiring way she communicates her ideas."

In both of these examples, we offer our respect as an acknowledgment of praiseworthy qualities we see in others. We have been taught that respect is something that must be earned, not freely given.

In the Gandhian philosophy, however, respect is not necessarily synonymous with admiration or outstanding behavior. Respect toward ourselves and others is unconditional and is based in the unity of all life.

A form of this concept is found in all of the great religious traditions. It is called the Golden Rule or the ethic of reciprocity; it states simply but profoundly that we are to treat others the way we wish to be treated. This is the meaning of respect: to place as much value on the life of another as we do on our own life.

As human beings we are genetically and elementally connected. In addition, we are connected at a soul level. If we look into the heart of humanity, we will find qualities and ideals that are common to all of us. These include the desire to love and be loved, to give of ourselves, to be free, to be creatively fulfilled, to feel joy, and to experience community with others.

However, because of our diverse natures, we each have our unique ways of achieving those desires. In other words, just because humanity shares a common desire of wanting to be happy doesn't mean we're all going to experience our happiness in the same ways.

The Golden Rule, or ethic of reciprocity, asks us to treat others as we would wish to be treated. However, it doesn't mean that just because we like certain things others will like them too. For example, we might want to do something nice for a friend and think, "I love surprise parties, so I'll plan one for Mary." If it turns out that Mary doesn't like surprises, our good intentions will have failed to produce the desired results, and there will be frustration and disappointment for all concerned. Our aim then, is to treat others in ways that respect their individuality. This means seeing them for who they are, not who *we* are.

Please Understand Me

The following story is a fictionalized account of two people struggling to understand one another. I have seen many similar situations during my years as a spiritual counselor, and I wanted to use this archetype to illustrate some common misperceptions that frequently cause difficulties in human relationships. The names Helen and Phil are also fictitious, but the dynamics in this familiar tale are very real.

Some years ago I counseled a couple who were feeling misunderstood by one another. Helen enjoyed interacting with people. She had a large group of friends and loved to entertain them as often as possible. Phil, her partner, enjoyed spending quiet evenings at home. He loved to read and had a large collection of books in their home library. Whenever Helen gave parties, Phil would show up for a few minutes and then politely retreat to a quiet place in another part of the house.

After they had been living together for several years, Helen became aware that Phil was spending more and more time by himself. Assuming he was bored, or perhaps depressed, Helen decided that

Phil needed more social interaction. After all, she reasoned, didn't she always perk up when she went out and had a good time with her friends?

Helen began insisting that Phil stay longer at their parties and mingle with others. She also arranged that they attend more social events so that he wouldn't feel cooped up in the house.

When Phil became even more withdrawn, Helen became more anxious to fix his problem. One day she decided that Phil would be happier if he spent more social time with his co-workers. She decided to sign Phil up to play in his office bowling league.

When Phil found out what Helen had done, he was furious and lost his temper. They became embroiled in a loud and lengthy argument, during which Phil told Helen that she was disrespecting him and trying to control his life. Helen accused Phil of disrespecting her and trying to shut her out. Phil called Helen a relentless nag and insisted that she give him his space. They hadn't spoken in several days.

When we met in my office, Helen was in tears and couldn't understand why Phil had treated her so badly. She said she loved him dearly and only wanted him to be happy. Phil apologized for his outburst and tried to explain that he was feeling overwhelmed by being forced to interact with so many people on a regular basis. He felt compelled to withdraw into himself in order to stay sane. Phil went on to say that he was happiest when he could spend some time alone every day to relax and read and occasionally have a quiet evening with a few friends.

It took a while for Helen to fully understand that she was inadvertently disrespecting Phil by insisting that what made her happy should also make him happy.

I asked them both to read the book *Please Understand Me*, written by David Keirsey and Marilyn Bates, which emphasizes that people's personality styles differ from one another. These differences do not make anyone right or wrong but need to be acknowledged so that we can increase our level of self-awareness and learn to interact with one another more respectfully. I then asked them to take the Keirsey

Temperament Sorter, which is a questionnaire to determine which values are most important to us as individuals. As I had predicted, Helen tested as an extrovert and Phil was a strong introvert.

The results truly amazed them both, and by studying the concepts in the book they came to see the importance of understanding different personality types. Helen learned that being an introvert is not an excuse for ignoring people. It is simply a more reserved way of looking at the world and deserves to be respected for what it is. Phil also gained new respect for Helen when he realized that, instead of being a control freak, she was just happier being with people and assumed that everyone felt the same way.

After several months of regular counseling sessions, Helen and Phil began to practice new ways of respecting one another. Helen became willing to host fewer parties, and Phil offered to attend them more frequently. As time went on, he became more open to sharing his feelings with her, and she learned how to give him the space he needed without fearing that something was wrong with him.

The last I heard, Phil and Helen were still together, enjoying a healthier and more loving relationship. He is still an introvert, and she is still an extrovert. Their personalities did not change. The big shift in consciousness occurred when they each chose to respect the other's differences. Now they work on accepting one another and demonstrating their love by participating in an ongoing process of give and take.

Real and lasting peace in relationships does not require that we always agree with one another. This is probably the most challenging principle to grasp about a culture of peace, because people tend to equate the idea of unity with uniformity. When we learn we don't have to give up our fundamental freedoms to live in peace, and we realize that diversity is an inherent part of unity, we can begin to understand what it really means to *live and let live*. Just as a symphony orchestra produces harmony by playing different instruments in tune, so it is that our world functions best when we give ourselves permission to express our own individuality and allow others to do the same.

How Do We Practice Respect?

We demonstrate our respect toward others by extending to them the same considerations we desire for ourselves. For example, if we want our voices to be heard, we will listen to the voices of others. If we want the freedom to disagree with opposing viewpoints, we will permit others to disagree with ours. If we want to love and marry whom we choose, we will allow others the same right. If we want to worship in a way that comforts us, we will welcome others to do the same. If we want to eat when we are hungry, we will take action to help feed others. This is the fundamental concept of the Golden Rule, and we can apply it to every area of our lives.

We demonstrate respect for ourselves by honoring our right to live in peace and harmony and choosing to live in accordance with our highest values. This means not only that we do all we can to support those values but that we will stand strong in the face of those who attempt to deny us those rights.

Remember, nonviolence is not the same as nonaction. It is just a different kind of action, one that does not harm others but makes it clear that we will not cooperate with any idea that demeans or denies our basic human rights.

As an evolving peacemaker,

I walk the path of

respect.

We must understand who we are, what we are, and why we are here on this earth. We are not born by accident. We are here for a purpose. And it is not a selfish purpose. It is a purpose of creating a world of peace and harmony.[31]

Arun Gandhi

---

[31] Matthew J. Evans, *A Quest For Peace: Nonviolence Among Religions* (WGIFilms, 2012)

Chapter 19

Understanding Our Purpose

U nderstanding involves much more than the accumulation of knowledge. It is our inherent ability to apply what we know to everyday living. When we fully understand something, we can make sense of it and become aware of our relationship to it.

Knowledge provides us with information. Understanding adds the component of clarity, which enhances our ability to find meaning and purpose in what we know. Opportunities to understand ourselves in relation to the world around us begin when we are very young.

For example, from the time we are toddlers we are warned again and again about what is safe and what is not. Generally speaking, our parents and teachers are very concerned for our well-being and tell us again and again not to use sharp objects, stick our fingers into electrical outlets, or burn ourselves on hot appliances. After they warn us about what not to do, they invariably add, "Do you understand?" and wait for us to dutifully reply yes. Even if we really don't understand what they said, we feel required to say yes so they will put the topic to rest.

Too often we assume we understand things and are more than a little surprised to find out there is much more to learn about the subject. Real understanding involves maturity, good judgment, and the ability to look beyond appearances instead of making assumptions. It is a process that takes time, attention, and a willingness to learn from our mistakes.

I first became conscious of the difference between knowledge and understanding when I was about three years old. I didn't know how to define it for a long time afterward, but the experience made an indelible impact on me.

I remember sitting at our kitchen table one afternoon watching my mother boil some water in a small pot. After a few minutes, the phone rang. She turned off the gas, moved the pot to the back burner, and went into the living room to answer the call. When I realized my mom would be occupied for a while, I casually strolled over to the gas range. I couldn't see the top of it, so I got the step stool to get a better view. From my new vantage point I could look down at the four black burners resting on top of the white enamel and was very impressed with my new discovery.

Since the gas was turned off, I assumed the burners were safe to touch. I really wanted to know what they felt like. Eagerly I put both hands, palms down, on the same front burner my mom had been using. In that shocking moment I realized that even though the gas was turned off, the burner was still terribly hot.

I screamed as the heat scalded my skin. In the next moment my mom came running into the kitchen. I don't remember too much after that except for the searing pain in my palms and lots of cold water running through my fingers. Of course my mom was a wreck, and even though my burns were superficial, she redoubled her efforts to keep me safe by not letting me out of her sight for a long time.

The gas burner experience made a tremendous impression on me. I had known enough to stay away from a burning flame but had not understood that a burner could stay hot even after the fire was turned off. This, like many life experiences to come, was painful but important to my growth and development.

In the weeks following this incident, I made some significant changes in my behavior. My parents remembered that I got into the habit of asking a lot of questions about how things worked before I attempted to touch or play with them. I began to see that my environment was much more complicated than it appeared to be on the surface.

As children we all go through such experiences, in an effort to satisfy our innate curiosity about the world around us. Each year that passes presents us with more opportunities to learn ways of navigating appropriately and safely in our environment.

Soon we find ourselves interacting with increasingly complex devices that come with instruction manuals. Too often, however, we don't understand the instructions. Other times we skim through the manual, assuming we know what to do, but then we find ourselves with a product that doesn't work and a handful of extra parts. These can be frustrating and time-consuming experiences. Our safest option is to take a deep breath, admit there is still more to understand, and then take time to read and reread the instructions.

Although human beings do not come with an instruction manual, we do have divine blueprints, written in our souls, which provide each of us with the capacity to understand the complexities of our own nature. Sometimes the blueprints can appear difficult to interpret. Other times we may assume to know who we are and what our purpose is, only to end up confused and frustrated. Nevertheless, we need to take the time to learn more of what the blueprints contain. We should begin with the premise that there is much more to us than what appears on the surface.

Who We Are

As we have discussed in previous chapters, we are all interconnected as a human family. We are individualized creations of the One Universal Omnipresent Spirit of Love, Life, and Wisdom. We come from the same Source, yet we each have our unique ways of expressing ourselves. This is an important part of the divine paradox; it's called "diversity within unity." Out of the One come the many and varied expressions of life.

This is perhaps the most challenging philosophical concept to really understand. As human beings, we often seem to be torn apart by our different ways of worshipping, different political views, and different sets of values, which seem to accentuate the fact that we have nothing in common. However, as we have already established, there is much more to who we are than what we appear to be. The truth is that we are all profoundly connected to one another by virtue of creation, and what happens to one of us has an impact on all of us. We are not required to agree with one another, but we do need to understand how and why it is necessary to coexist without attempting to destroy each other out of fear and ignorance.

It has been said that we are spiritual beings learning to be fully human. This makes sense to me, because we are spiritual and whole by nature. Yet at a human level we have much to learn and are still getting burned by what we don't understand. This is part of our learning process and invariably presents us with opportunities to experience greater understanding.

Our Purpose

All creation begins in our minds. Each of us has been given a rich storehouse of creative ideas that have the potential to contribute to a more peaceful and harmonious environment. These ideas, hopes, and dreams are part of our divine blueprint. Every piece of art, every invention, every cure for a disease, every act of love has begun as an idea. These ideas are within every one of us and are not created by accident. It is our responsibility to recognize them for what they are, develop them, and bring them forth into our environment to create a world of peace. Ideas are God's gift to us, and expressing them is our gift to the world.

Once we understand that we are here for a purpose, we are more inclined to express our individuality. As Arun has stated, this is not a selfish purpose. Too often we diminish our own importance, because we feel insecure about our talents. However, we need to understand that our unique gifts of the Spirit are as valuable to God as the most cherished jewel on the planet. Keeping that jewel to ourselves deprives the world of something pure and precious. Letting our light shine and encouraging others to do the same brings hope to a world badly in need of healing. We can never know how many lives we touch

173

just by being who we were created to be. As we learn to respect and understand humanity in the light of our highest potential, we will become more willing to reach out to one another and honor the spiritual gifts inherent within each one of us.

Let us resolve to expand our horizons by learning to understand more about other cultures, lifestyles, religions, and political viewpoints. Let us compare and contrast, without condemnation, the similarities and differences between other points of view and our own. Let us make a greater effort to respectfully communicate with those whose beliefs are different from ours. Let us learn to understand more of the invincible power of love to heal and transform our lives.

As an evolving peacemaker,

I walk the path of

understanding.

When we accept each other as human beings we will not identify people with the labels we have put upon them.[32]

Arun Gandhi

[32]   Matthew J. Evans, *A Quest For Peace: Nonviolence Among Religions* (WGIFilms, 2012)

Chapter 20

Embracing Our Human Dignity

Have you ever been called unflattering names because of your height, weight, religion, skin color, occupation, lack of education, or lifestyle? Have you ever been referred to in demeaning terms because you or your ancestors have come from different countries or speak with accents? Have you ever heard the words "you people" directed at you in a derogatory way? Have you ever been refused service at a restaurant because of your ethnicity or whom you choose to love?

Too many people suffer these attacks of passive violence every day of their lives. Being labeled as inferior because of who we are generates feelings of shame that build up inside of us. The shame is usually followed by anger, and if we allow our anger to escalate, we often end up directing it toward others. This is a cycle of violence that tends to spread its poison from generation to generation and can only be healed when we learn to accept and appreciate one another.

Acceptance, in this context, is defined as our ability to value all individuals without prejudging them or classifying them as inferior. Appreciation is our expression of gratitude for what their journey through life can teach us.

When we are willing to accept and appreciate others as individuals, we open ourselves to a whole new world. By interacting with those who have come from different backgrounds or have overcome unique types of challenges, we often find powerful life lessons that can enrich and bless us.

Some of my earliest memories center around the stories my family told about coming to the United States from Eastern Europe in the early 1900s. I learned that they, along with so many others of their generation, were everyday heroes who had survived wars, persecution, poverty, and all manner of physical, mental, and emotional hardships just to stay alive. Their dream had been to come to America to be free.

When a few of my relatives actually arrived in the United States and made it through Ellis Island, they had another set of challenges. They had to work in sweatshops to save enough money to bring their relatives to this country. Even though they worked day and night, it often took as long as five years to purchase one steamship ticket. They had no formal education to speak of, yet they had the strength, wisdom, and compassion to take care of themselves and their families.

Some of my family members worked during the day and pursued an education by going to night school. Eventually they graduated from college and became professionals in their chosen fields. Others were apprentices to tradesmen and learned to become shoemakers, painters, or carpenters. My grandfather became a shoemaker who excelled at his craft.

Most of the women became wives and mothers and cared for their families without ever learning to read or write. My grandmother was one of those women.

If you looked at Grandma Sadie, you would see a simple woman without airs or pretenses of any kind. She did not dress to impress nor try to draw attention to herself. If you saw her on the street, she would likely be carrying shopping bags from the grocery store. If it was winter she would be wearing a head scarf and a woolen coat over a plain housedress. Most people who walked past her would categorize her as a poor immigrant without much education. They would not necessarily go out of their way to get to know her because they would have already labeled and discounted her as nobody special.

However, those who knew my grandmother saw her as a hero. She and my grandpa Abe had very little money. They lived in a small apartment in back of their shoe repair shop. Yet Grandma Sadie was often compared to a magician, because she could take a small portion of food and make it last until she'd fed dozens of people who had nothing to eat. She would fill her shopping bags and travel hours by city bus to make sure a sick relative had a sweater and some hot soup.

She planted vegetable gardens in her small backyard, where the soil was so rocky and malnourished that no one thought anything would survive there. Nevertheless, it seemed that every seed she planted thrived. When a pregnant neighbor was in labor with no one to care for her, Grandma delivered the baby and kept the newborn safe and warm until help arrived.

In addition to raising two children and tending to all the household chores, Grandma worked from home, weaving hair into switches. I used to marvel at how fast her fingers would fly across the weaving board. She would receive dozens of boxes of unwoven hair from the hair-goods manufacturer and within the week would send the finished products back to them. Grandma was paid by the piece and had to perform her tasks quickly and accurately. She worked hard at that job for long hours every day to provide a few extras for my mother and uncle.

Left to right: my mother, Sophie; Grandpa Abe;
Uncle Harry; and Grandma Sadie, circa 1938

When my mother wanted piano lessons, Grandma made sure she had them. After years of study, my mother became an accomplished piano teacher. When my uncle Harry studied in another city to get his PhD, Grandma made long commutes to ensure he had enough to eat so that he wouldn't despair and quit school. Some years later he became a world renowned chemist with over 150 patents to his credit.

Grandma was no ordinary woman. She was a highly intelligent and capable person whose life reflected her love, wisdom, and boundless generosity. The same is true for a great many women and men throughout the world who have made extraordinary but little-known contributions to the lives of others. We probably will never meet most of them nor have the opportunity to get to know them. However, the next time we happen to encounter an "ordinary" person or someone who is "different," let us remember not to be fooled by appearances. These people are individuals who have loved, suffered, triumphed, and survived. Let us make an effort to listen to their stories and learn to appreciate their journeys.

As we choose to accept others, we learn to respect their unique talents and spiritual gifts. We no longer regard them as expendable, nor do we attempt to categorize them into groups who all think and feel the same way. Instead, we come to appreciate their individual value and, by doing so, enhance our collective value as citizens of the world.

As an evolving peacemaker,

I walk the path of

acceptance and appreciation.

Epilogue

Prelude to Peace

Respect will never come through anger, aggression, shootings, and all the divisive dialogue that violence generates. Respect will come through education, through broadening our perspectives, through friendly dialogue and most importantly through honest admission that we are prejudiced—every one of us of whatever race, and be willing to take necessary peaceful measures to eradicate the hate.

Arun Gandhi

This past week two hate crimes against minority groups have made the news, and another terrorist attack has taken place. The collective shadow of humanity has forced its way through the barricade of denial and is striking out with the unresolved rage of generations. We are being inundated with the harsher realities we have been unwilling or unable to acknowledge until now. Everywhere we look we see evidence of prejudice, racism, terrorism, fear, disrespect, and greed. We are horrified—and rightly so. This is the culture of violence that has been part of the collective consciousness of humanity for a very long time. Now is the time to face these issues and do everything in our power to help heal them. Now is when our work really begins.

Let us make an effort to engage in sincere and amicable dialogue with people whose points of view might differ from our own.

Let us become affiliated with organizations that are focused on putting an end to all forms of discrimination.

Let us write and phone our elected officials on a regular basis and let them know which issues we want them to support.

Let us educate our children by teaching them to respect our planet and every member of our human family

Let us write books, paint pictures, produce films, sing songs, volunteer our time to worthy causes, and gather together often to celebrate the power of unity and love.

Let us make our voices heard around the world and honor the heroes who have paved the way for us to walk the path of the evolving peacemaker.

Remember, it is not by searching for peace but by *being* the peace that we honor our commitment to nonviolence. Welcome to the journey.

As an evolving peacemaker I walk the path of

New Beginnings
Courage
Hope
Patience
Creativity
Global Awareness
Nonviolent Action
Self-Discovery
Inner Healing
Self-Discipline
Healthy Self-Expression
Humility
Self-Acceptance
Emotional Intelligence
Forgiving Others
Self-Forgiveness
Love
Unity with All Life
Respect
Understanding
Acceptance and Appreciation.

Questions for Discussion

Do you belong to a book club in which you can discuss the following questions with other members of your group, or do you prefer to process your thoughts through private journaling? Either way, we invite you study the questions that pertain to each chapter. Take time every day to become quiet, and meditate on the ideas that are most meaningful to you. As you work with these teachings, you will gain a greater awareness of your own spiritual power and continue to discover how many ways one person can make a difference.

If you are interested in starting a study group or book club in your area and would like our support, please feel free to contact us. Every seed we plant in the name of nonviolence makes a difference.

Please remember: our mission involves learning to embrace nonviolence as a way of life. We do this by walking the path of the *evolving peacemaker*.

Chapter 1

My First Encounter with Violence

1) When you were growing up, were you ever attacked or harassed by those who believed you were different or inferior? Explain.

2) Did you seek help from others? What was the outcome?

3) How were you affected by those experiences? What did you learn?

4) Since you have experienced the pain of being harassed, do you feel more compassionate toward people who are discriminated against on a daily basis? What can you do to support them?

Notes

Chapter 2

Searching for Truth

1) Was religion an important part of your childhood? Have your beliefs changed over the years? If so, how?

2) Have you ever studied world religions or been involved with faiths different from your own? What have you learned from your studies?

3) Do you make a distinction between religion and spirituality? If so, what do you see as the similarities and differences?

4) How do you relate with those who try to convince you that their religion is the only true religion?

5) Discuss your vision for peace in the world.

Notes

Chapters 3 and 4

One Person at a Time and A Quest for Peace

1) What did Arun's words "One person at a time" mean to you?

2) Tell about a time when a small act of kindness lifted your spirits and offered you hope for the future.

3) Give examples of everyday heroes who are making a positive difference one person at time.

4) Share three occasions when you brightened someone's day. Take a moment to reflect on how much of a difference you can make in someone's life.

5) Discuss some of your favorite and most memorable films. How and why did they touch you so deeply?

Notes

Chapter 5

An Invitation to the United Nations

1) What did you learn about the United Nations that you didn't know before?

2) Has your opinion of the UN changed after reading this chapter? If so, how?

3) Ambassador Chowdhury said, "If you provide young people a voice, a platform, or a medium like filmmaking, you have made a contribution to the culture of peace." How do you interpret his statement? In what ways can you help give young people a voice?

4) Discuss a time when you encouraged a child or teen to believe that his or her voice mattered.

5) How do you think the arts can contribute to a culture of peace? What types of art or music inspire and uplift you?

Notes

Chapter 6

Satyagraha: A Philosophy of Nonviolence

1) Discuss the Grain of Wheat story. How does the second sage describe the meaning of peace? How does this idea differ from the popular belief that we can only experience peace by removing ourselves from the intrusions of everyday life?

2) Share your understanding of satyagraha. How did Gandhi describe the difference between passive resistance and nonviolent resistance?

3) Martin Luther King said that Gandhi believed love was a "potent instrument for social and collective transformation." How do you believe love can provide the foundation for social reform?

4) This chapter lists Gandhi's guidelines for those who would practice satyagraha. Discuss ways that Gandhi and his followers applied those ideas during the Salt March. In what ways do you see the practice of satyagraha being effective in today's world?

5) Share a time when you planted a seed of peace. In what ways did you see it grow?

Notes

Chapter 7

The Many Faces of Passive Violence

1) Discuss occasions when you've seen passive violence turn into physical violence. What do you think could have been done differently to generate a nonviolent outcome?

2) Are there certain words that were used against you when you were growing up that still generate painful memories? What can you do to help heal that pain?

3) How often do you get angry with yourself for not meeting you own expectations? How do you use passive violence against yourself?

4) Have you ever bullied someone? What were your reasons? What was the outcome?

5) Discuss Gandhi's statement, "If we want to teach real peace in this world we should start by educating children." What are some ways we can help our children learn to be more compassionate with one another?

Notes

Chapter 8

The Gift of Self-Knowledge

1) Why is self-knowledge so important to our spiritual growth and development?

2) What types of criticism cause you to feel most vulnerable? Why do you believe you are particularly sensitive in those areas?

3) Discuss an occasion when you tried to give someone constructive criticism and they became defensive toward you. How did it feel to hear that your intentions were misunderstood? What did you do about it?

4) Share your understanding of self-observation. How are you working toward becoming more objective with your self-talk? Give examples of how you are changing your inner dialogue.

5) In chapter 8 we read, "What we do is subject to evaluation and improvement. Who we are is always enough." Discuss how this idea can help you become more open to receiving input from others.

Notes

Chapter 9

Shedding Light on Anger

1) What were you taught about anger during your formative years? Were you permitted to speak your mind during disagreements or advised to keep quiet?

2) How do you typically cope with anger? Have your methods changed much since you were a child?

3) Discuss Gandhi's statement, "An eye for an eye ends in making everybody blind."

4) What did Grandfather Gandhi wish to convey to Arun when he said that anger is like lightning? Do you agree with Gandhi's definition? Explain.

5) Tell of a time when someone inadvertently pushed one of your buttons and you expressed anger you didn't realize was inside of you. How important is it to come to terms with our hidden anger?

Notes

Chapter 10

Turning Lightning into a Lamp

1) Share a time when you were treated unjustly and felt angry and betrayed. How did you handle it? Are you still carrying some residual anger you would like to heal?

2) In Chapter 10 we read, "There are certain things in life we can control and certain things we can't control." Why is this a valuable lesson in anger management?

3) How often have you invested your time and energy in trying to make something happen that was beyond your control? What has been your biggest lesson from these efforts?

4) How does the phrase "this or something better" encourage you to keep moving in a positive direction despite obstacles or disappointments?

5) Give an example of when you made the choice to "turn lightning into a lamp." How did you use your energy in constructive ways?

Notes

Chapter 11

The Consequences of Concealed Anger

1) Which of the passive-aggressive characteristics on the list in chapter 11 do you relate to the most?

2) How often do you try to express your concerns to others in indirect ways? Have these attempts been successful in getting your needs met?

3) What holds you back from expressing your true feelings more often?

4) Share an example from your own life of a time when behavior modification alone was not enough to make a permanent change in your life. Did you discover underlying anger that needed to be addressed before a healing could take place? What motivated you to eventually make the change you were working toward?

5) In chapter 11 we read, "It was easy to see passive-aggressive behavior in those around me, and it was even easier to criticize it. However, my biggest insight occurred one day when I realized that the behaviors I was criticizing in others were the same ones I needed to heal in myself!" How can you use this insight to help improve the quality of your relationships and manage your anger more effectively?

Notes

Chapter 12

The Art of Self-Acceptance

1) Share your understanding of self-acceptance. Why is it so important on our journey toward a culture of peace? Can we really accept others without accepting ourselves?

2) How is self-acceptance different from self-approval and self-justification? Why is it so important to be honest with ourselves?

3) Discuss the shadow side of the human consciousness. Where does the shadow come from? How do we feed our shadow when we deny our own reality?

4) Discuss the concept of projection. Give examples of how groups and communities project their dark sides onto others and turn them into scapegoats and enemies.

5) What character traits do you believe you have buried most deeply inside yourself? How can you begin to embrace and accept them?

Notes

Chapter 13

Social and Emotional Intelligence

1) Review the list of attributes associated with high social and emotional intelligence (SEI). Which of them are you strong in? Which do you want to develop in yourself?

2) How does high SEI enhance business and personal relationships? How can it improve the quality of your own interactions with others?

3) In chapter 13 we read that developing emotional maturity helps us "identify and heal limiting beliefs from our past that have contributed to shaping our worldview." What negative or limiting beliefs were you taught as a child? Were you ever taught that certain groups of people were inferior? Did family members or teachers convince you that you lacked the talent to achieve your goals? When did you realize those beliefs were not true? Are you still working on healing some of those issues from your past?

4) Why is it important to value both our intellectual and emotional intelligence rather than emphasizing one over the other?

5) Discuss which of the SEI attributes is most relevant to you at this time.

Notes

Chapter 14

With Malice toward None

1) Share a time when you denied your feelings after being hurt by someone and inadvertently built up more resentment. How did you come to terms with the situation?

2) Was there an occasion when you felt you could not forgive someone because they did not apologize or take responsibility for their actions? Are you still feeling resentment about it? If so, what steps are you taking to heal those feelings?

3) Discuss a time when you offered an apology to someone and they did not accept it. Have you forgiven them for not forgiving you?

4) Discuss the concept of agreeing to disagree. How can you put this idea to work in your personal and professional relationships?

5) Are there people in your life you haven't forgiven? What steps are you willing to take to heal those issues?

Notes

Chapter 15

The Forgiving Power of Love

1) Why is it important to forgive yourself? How can self-forgiveness help to bring aspects of your shadow into the light?

2) How did Willie's correspondence with Sis help him reach a new level of self-awareness? What did she see in him that he couldn't see in himself?

3) What do you find hard to forgive in yourself? How does Willie's story give you inspiration to release self-condemnation?

4) How do Willie's experiences help you understand that everyone is worthy of being forgiven?

5) When Willie was young, he thought being tough would make him a hero. He finally became a hero through the power of love. Share your thoughts on this statement.

Notes

Chapter 16

Ahimsa: Heaven on Earth

1) In what ways does the concept of ahimsa encompass more than the avoidance of physical force?

2) How did Gandhi demonstrate ahimsa toward those who were labeled as "untouchables?"

3) How did Gandhi's advice to Souren Bannerji reveal the power of ahimsa to overcome tragedy with love?

4) Share a time when you felt the power of ahimsa (unconditional love) produce a significant change in your life.

5) In what area of your life does the practice of ahimsa present the greatest challenge? What can you do to bring more love into your life?

Notes

Chapter 17

Honoring Our Relationship with All Life

1) Explain how the genetic discoveries concerning the interrelatedness of all life can help us understand more about the concept of diversity within unity.

2) Discuss the genetic findings that prove there is only one race, the human race. Picture a world without racial prejudice. In what ways would things be different?

3) What are some of the ways you are reducing, reusing, and recycling? How can you continue to reduce your carbon footprint?

4) An important way we can experience interdependence is by learning to give generously and receive graciously. What are some of the consequences we are likely to face if we favor one practice over the other?

Notes

Chapter 18

Do Unto Others

1) Gandhi believed that respect toward ourselves and others is unconditional and based on the Golden Rule. Discuss how this point of view differs from the traditional notion that respect must be earned.

2) Share examples of when you had differences with others because you saw them as *you* were and not as *they* were.

3) In chapter 18 we read "...people tend to equate the idea of unity with uniformity." How does this idea help you relate to others?

4) How can we show respect toward others?

5) How can we show respect for ourselves?

Notes

Chapter 19

Understanding Our Purpose

1) Discuss the difference between knowledge and understanding.

2) Share a time (without blame or shame) when your lack of understanding caused you to make an assumption about someone or something that proved to be incorrect or even damaging. What was the outcome?

3) What do you understand about your divine blueprint? How is it the same as all others'? How is it different?

4) What efforts are you making to understand more about the beliefs and lifestyles of others? What would you like others to understand about you?

5) How does understanding others help you respect them more?

Notes

Chapter 20

Embracing Our Human Dignity

1) Discuss a time when you took for granted or underestimated someone who was really an everyday hero. How did you learn to see his or her value?

2) Did you ever disregarded someone's intelligence because he or she was not formally educated? Did you learn to accept and appreciate this person? How did the change take place?

3) Have you ever felt unaccepted and unappreciated because you did not measure up to the standards of others? How did you handle the situation?

4) Do you feel you have more appreciation for others as a result of your own experiences with rejection?

5) Discuss ways you can practice accepting and appreciating others as individuals rather than stereotyping or labeling them.

Notes

Acknowledgments

Matthew and I extend our heartfelt thanks to Arun Gandhi, one of the great leaders of the international peace movement. His wisdom, generosity, and willingness to support our work has been a great blessing to us. He is a wonderful role model, a great humanitarian, and a loving friend.

We would also like to thank Ruth Cherry and Susan Stewart for their meticulous and insightful editing of our manuscript and talented artist Linda Mercer, who recognized the symbolism in a grain of wheat and created our beautiful cover art. Much love and thanks to Terri Keefer Photography and Genesis Keefer for our amazing headshots.

We are most grateful to our spiritual family at Unity of San Luis Obispo, California, who gave us their unwavering support and continued to believe in our project in spite of countless rewrites, revisions, and delays. Some of these "evolving peacemakers" include Sharon Mesker; Lou, Jeanne, and Kathy Silva; Joan G. Sargen; Francesca Nemko; Dorothy Schwartz; Rick and Dixie Ridge; Keith Hamilton; Sharie Rouse; Marilee and Frank Taylor; Karen Wilkins; TeaEster Higgins; Linda Perkins; Patricia Rogers Gordon; Mary Vickers; Valerie Nevo; Claudia Davis; Shirley Polich; Ann and Don Aronson; Mike and Joyce Heller; Donna and Debra Mason; Betty Kittel; Edie Juck; John Kert and Sandy Allen; Janice, Mike, Sophy, and Hannah Kelsey; Barbara Lane; Mike Mesker; Kevin Casey; Paula Motlo; Gary Stone; Carolyn Towery; Evelyn Beaule; Brett and Julia Mitchell; Nancy Woodard; Sapphire Grace; P. J. Schrotel; Patty

Hayes; Sheri Hatch; Joyce Bayless; Mary and Ron Gabel; and Alan and Marylou Varni.

Our sincere thanks to Willie Bermudez for sharing his inspiring story of redemption and teaching us how the power of love can change lives.

We also send our heartfelt appreciation to Dr. Kamalesh Kumar Sankhala and Dr. Nicholas Bernthal at UCLA for their medical expertise and compassionate support during Leona's illness in 2015.

Last, but certainly not least, we are deeply grateful to Mahatma Gandhi, whose life and teachings have inspired us to live our lives as evolving peacemakers.

About the Authors

Leona Evans holds a Master of Arts in Religious Studies. She is an ordained Unity Minister, spiritual counselor, and former Chair of the Metaphysics Department at Unity School for Religious Studies. She is the co-author, with Carol Keefer, of two books: *Nothing Is Too Good to Be True!* which was also translated and published in Russia, and *Spirituality & Self-Esteem*. In addition, she co-authored and narrated a two-CD set, *Meditations for Transformation: Awakening the Soul through the Enneagram.*

Ordained in 1985, Evans has been the minister at Unity of San Luis Obispo, California, for the past twenty-two years, during which time she has taught numerous classes on the power of the mind to shape our destiny. Leona is an accomplished speaker and teacher, and her positive messages have been heard on radio and television stations throughout the world.

Evans is a former Broadway actress, recording artist, and cabaret performer, whose theatrical career of more than thirty years began when she was a small child. Eventually she was guided to study world religions and chose the ministry as a way of helping people understand that nonviolence among religions begins with the realization that the same God of love indwells all people.

Evans is the proud mother of musician, filmmaker, and actor Matthew J. Evans, whose rich contributions to this volume have added "author" to his considerable list of accomplishments.

Leona is available to present her workshops and seminars at business conferences, spiritual centers, and educational venues.

An accomplished actor, musician, and award-winning young filmmaker, **Matthew J. Evans** was born in 1996 and is a native of San Luis Obispo, California. He played a feature role in Columbia Pictures' comedy *Bad Teacher*, for which he received a 2012 Young Artist Award in Los Angeles. A frequent guest star on a number of network television shows, Matthew appeared on the Disney XD series *Lab Rats* in 2014, for which he won another Young Artist Award. In 2015, he played a dramatic role in the feature film *Dismissed*.

A professional musician, Matthew sings and plays double bass, acoustic guitar, and bass guitar. He is also a documentary filmmaker whose mission is to produce movies and videos that entertain, educate, and inspire audiences to find value and meaning in their lives and in the world.

In 2010 Matthew produced and directed a short film called *A War Story, A Love Story*, which won Best Documentary and Best in Festival at Interlochen Future of Cinema International Film Festival.

In 2011 Matthew produced and directed a documentary short film called *Poetic Justice Project*, which won Best Student Documentary at the Spirit Quest Film Festival in Pennsylvania, Best Young Filmmaker Documentary Short at the Red Rock Film Festival in Utah, and, in 2014, the Gold Jury Prize at the Social Justice Film Festival, Youth Visions Competition in Seattle.

In 2012 Matthew produced and directed a documentary short film called *A Quest For Peace: Nonviolence Among Religions*, featuring interviews with Arun Gandhi, grandson of Mahatma Gandhi. During 2013–14, the film won awards at nineteen film festivals throughout the country.

A highlight of Matthew's filmmaking career was receiving the first Teen Art of Making Peace Award in September 2014 from the Peace in the Streets Global Film Festival, presented to him at the United Nations third High Level Forum on a Culture of Peace by Former Under-Secretary-General Anwarul Chowdhury.

Author, speaker, humanitarian, and renowned peace activist **Arun Gandhi** has devoted his life to the philosophy of nonviolence as taught to him by his legendary grandfather, Mahatma Gandhi.

Arun says he's frequently asked if Mahatma Gandhi's teachings are relevant today. "His philosophies are based on love, respect, and understanding. If we question whether his philosophies are relevant, we question whether love, respect, and understanding are relevant."

Arun calls himself a peace farmer: "Just as a farmer goes out into the fields and plants seeds and hopes and prays that he gets a good crop, I just go out and plant seeds and pray that those seeds will germinate."

Made in the USA
San Bernardino, CA
19 January 2018